UN**FAIR**

Other Books by John Shore

*I'm OK–You're Not: The Message We're Sending
Nonbelievers and Why We Should Stop*

*"Penguins, Pain and the Whole Shebang: Why I Do
the Things I Do," by God (as told to John Shore)*

Hell No! Extinguishing Christian Hellfire

10 Ways (We) Christians Fail to be Christian

*Seven Reasons Women Stay in Abusive Relationships
and How To Defeat Each One of Them*

HA!

Comma Sense: A FUNdamental Guide to Punctuation

UNFAIR

CHRISTIANS AND THE LGBT QUESTION

JOHN SHORE

To every gay person who has ever, in any way, received the message that God is grieved by their sexual orientation.

And to my wife Catherine, a genius at seeing straight to the heart of everything.

Acknowledgements

A deep and heartfelt thanks to Dan Wilkinson, Dan Savage, Rob Bell, Daren Erisman, Paul Rauchenbush, Jay Bakker, Ross Murray, Gwen Ashby, Joe Jervis, Roger McClellan, Randy Roberts Potts, Diane Reischling, Sarah Stelfox, John Baker, Gwen Hernandez, and all the gang at Unfundamentalist Christians.

Contents

Introduction

A while back I received an email from a young Christian lesbian who wanted nothing more than to come out to her Southern Baptist parents. But she knew that doing so would likely destroy her relationship with them. This earnest, honest, loving daughter was torn between being true to herself, and "absolutely devastating" the two people in the world who mean the most to her.

"I know what would happen if I told them about who I really am," she wrote. "They would be so, so hurt; and I would never be at peace from their efforts to 'save' me. ... I can't believe this is what my life has turned into. How did modern Christianity get so [expletive deleted] that a totally average girl like me, from an otherwise great family, has to feel this kind of pain, and cause my parents to feel it, too?"

After picking my heart up off the floor, I thought, "How can people read letters like this and ever doubt that a person can be both gay and Christian?"

The problem, I realized, was that people *weren't* reading such letters, because, as far as I knew, no collection of them had ever been published.

So, via a post on my blog, JohnShore.com, titled, *Gay Christians: Tell the World Your Story*, I put out a call for gay and lesbian Christians to send me their stories. You now hold in your hands a selection of the over three hundred responses I received.

I think these gut-wrenching yet profoundly inspirational testimonials are vital to our understanding of the proper relationship between LGBT people and Christianity. Because if it's true that gay people can be, and are, just as Christian as anyone else, then I don't see any way to avoid the conclusion that there must be something erroneous with the assumption that the God whom Christians worship finds gay people morally repelling.

Popular Christian opinion once held that the Bible condoned both slavery and the prohibition of women's suffrage. Is it such a stretch to now reconsider the conviction that God finds being gay, in and of itself, offensive?

Read these letters and see what you think.

Preceding the letters is my essay, *Taking God at His Word: The Bible and Homosexuality*, which makes a complete and I believe conclusive case for why the Christian condemnation of gay relationships is not only egregiously unfair, but manifestly unbiblical. Following the letters are a dozen or so of my own most influential shorter essays on the matter generally.

Yours in the belief that God is equally fair to all,

John Shore

One of the teachers of the law came and heard them debating. Noticing that Jesus had given them a good answer, he asked him, "Of all the commandments, which is the most important?"

"The most important one," answered Jesus, "is this: 'Hear, O Israel: The Lord our God, the Lord is one. Love the Lord your God with all your heart and with all your soul and with all your mind and with all your strength.' The second is this: 'Love your neighbor as yourself.' There is no commandment greater than these."

(Mark 12:28-31)

There is neither Jew nor Greek, slave nor free, male nor female, for you are all one in Christ Jesus.

(Galatians 3:28)

Taking God at His Word: The Bible and Homosexuality

God does not ask us to choose between compassion and faith in the Bible.

Christians are increasingly divided over the issue of the acceptance and inclusion of gay persons into the church. The debate itself is usually framed as essentially pitting the Bible, on one hand, against compassion and social justice on the other. Our Christian hearts, runs the (usually impassioned) argument, compel us to grant full moral and legal equality to gay and lesbian people; our Christian faith, comes the (usually impassioned) rebuttal, compels us to cleave, above all, to the word of God.

Compassion for others is the fundamental cornerstone of Christian ethics; the Bible is the bedrock of the Christian faith. What Christian can possibly choose between the two?

The answer is that no Christian is called upon to make that choice. The text of the Bible on one hand, and full equality for gay and lesbian people on the other, is a false dichotomy. God would not ask or expect Christians to ever choose between their compassion and their faith.

Reconciling the Bible with unqualified acceptance and equality for LGBT people does not necessitate discounting, recasting, or deconstructing the Bible. All it takes is reading those passages of the Bible wherein homosexuality is mentioned with the same care that we would any other passage of the book.

We can trust God; we can trust that God is loving.

And we can trust that we can—and that we certainly should—take God, in this matter, as in all things, at his word.

If there is no clearly stated directive in the Bible to marginalize and ostracize gay people, then it is morally indefensible for Christians to continue to do so.

What cannot be denied is that Christians have caused a great deal of pain and suffering to gay persons, by:

- Banning their participation in the church, thus depriving them of the comforts and spiritual fruits of the church.

- Banning their participation in the sacrament of marriage, thus depriving them of the comforts and spiritual fruits of marriage.

- Damaging the bonds between gays and their straight family members, thus weakening the comforts and spiritual fruits of family life for both gays and their families.

- Using their position within society as spokespersons for God to proclaim that all homosexual relations are disdained by God, thus knowingly contributing to the cruel persecution of a minority population.

Christians do not deny that they have done these things. However, they contend that they have no choice *but* to do these things, based on what they say is a clear directive about homosexuals delivered to them by God through the Holy Bible. They assert that the Bible defines all homosexual acts as sinful, instructs them to exclude from full participation in the church all non-repentant sinners (including gay people), and morally calls upon them to publicly (or at least resolutely) denounce homosexual acts.

Without an explicit directive from God to exclude and condemn homosexuals, the Christian community's treatment of gay persons is in clear violation of what Jesus and the New Testament writers pointedly identified as one-half of God's most important commandment: to love one's neighbor as one's self.

The gay community has cried out for justice from Christians, who have a biblically mandated obligation to be just. Because the suffering imposed on gay persons by Christians is so severe, the directive from God to marginalize and ostracize gay people would have to be *clear and explicit* in the Bible. If there is no such clearly stated directive, then the continued Christian mistreatment of gay and lesbian people is morally indefensible, and must cease.

Heterosexual Christians are being unbiblical by using the clobber passages as justification for applying absolute standards of morality to homosexual "sins" that they themselves are not tempted to commit, while at the same time accepting for themselves a standard of relative morality for those sins listed in the clobber passages that they *do* routinely commit.

Homosexuality is briefly mentioned in only six or seven of the Bible's 31,173 verses. (The verses wherein homosexuality is mentioned are commonly known as the "clobber passages," since they are typically used by Christians to "clobber" LGBT people.) The fact that homosexuality is so rarely mentioned in the Bible should be an indication to us of the lack of importance ascribed it by the authors of the Bible.

While the Bible is nearly silent on homosexuality, a great deal of its content is devoted to how a Christian should behave. Throughout, the New Testament insists upon fairness, equity, love, and the rejection of legalism over compassion. If heterosexual Christians are obligated to look to the Bible to determine the sinfulness of homosexual acts, how much greater is their obligation to look to the Bible to determine the sinfulness of their behavior *toward* gay persons, especially in light of the gay community's call to them for justice?

Some Bible passages pertinent to this concern are:

Let any one of you who is without sin be the first to throw a stone at her. (John 8:7)

Let no debt remain outstanding, except the continuing debt to love one another, for whoever loves others has fulfilled the law. The commandments, "You shall not commit adultery," "You shall not murder," "You shall not steal," "You shall not covet," and whatever other command there may be, are summed up in this one command: "Love your neighbor as yourself." Love does no harm to a neighbor. Therefore love is the fulfillment of the law. (Romans 13:8-10)

Here there is no Gentile or Jew, circumcised or uncircumcised, barbarian, Scythian, slave or free, but Christ is all, and is in all. Therefore, as God's chosen people, holy and dearly loved, clothe yourselves with compassion, kindness, humility, gentleness and patience. Bear with each other and forgive one another if any of you has a grievance against someone. Forgive as the Lord forgave you. (Colossians 3:11-13)

Woe to you, teachers of the law and Pharisees, you hypocrites! You give a tenth of your spices—mint, dill and cumin. But you have neglected the more important matters of the law—justice, mercy and faithfulness. You should have practiced the latter, without neglecting the former. You blind guides! You strain out a gnat but swallow a camel. (Matthew 23:23-24)

A fundamental tenet of Christianity is that we are all born sinners, that we have no choice but to exist in relationship to our sinful natures. And so Christians accept as inevitable that any given Christian will, for instance, on occasion drink too much, lust, or tell a lie.

As we've seen, in the clobber passages Paul also condemns, along with homosexuality, those three specific sins. But Christians don't think that they are expected to never commit *any* degree of those sins. They understand that circumstances and normal human weaknesses must be taken into account before condemning any transgression. We all readily understand and accept the moral distinction between drinking socially and being a drunk, between a lustful thought and committing adultery, between telling a flattering white lie and chronically lying.

Even a sin as heinous as murder we do not judge without first taking into account the context in which it occurred. Self-defense, protection of the innocent, during a war—we recognize that there are times when taking the life of another is not only *not* a sin, but a morally justified and even heroic act.

Christians evaluate the degree of sin, or even whether or not a real sin has occurred, by looking at both the harm caused by the sin, and the intent of the sin's perpetrator.

They do, that is, for all sins *except* homosexuality.

Virtually any degree of homosexual "transgression" gets treated by some Christians as an absolute sin deserving absolute punishment. Such Christians draw no moral distinction between the homosexual gang rape in the story of Sodom and Gomorrah, the orgies to which Paul refers in his letter to the Romans, the wild sexual abandon Paul addresses in 1 Corinthians, and consensual homosexual sex between loving and committed homosexual partners.

Heterosexual Christians are being unfair and hypocritical by using the clobber passages as justification for applying absolute standards of morality (and an absolute penalty) to homosexual "sins" that they themselves are never tempted to commit, while at the same time accepting for themselves a standard of relative morality (and applying no real penalty) for those sins listed in the clobber passages that they *do* routinely commit.

As there is no demonstrable harm arising from sex within a committed homosexual relationship, and there *is* significant demonstrable harm arising from the discrimination against and condemnation of gay persons, what possible biblical basis can there be for not recognizing the vast moral differences between sex acts done within the context of a loving committed relationship, and sex acts of any other sort?

Here are a couple of Bible passages that any Christian should bear in mind whenever he or she is called upon (or at least emotionally compelled) to render a moral judgment:

> Do not judge, or you too will be judged. For in the same way you judge others, you will be judged, and with the measure you use, it will be measured to you. (Matthew 7:1-2)

> Why do you look at the speck of sawdust in your brother's eye and pay no attention to the plank in your own eye? How can you say to your brother, 'Brother, let me take the speck out of your eye,' when you yourself fail to see the plank in your own eye? You hypocrite, first take the plank out of your eye, and then you will see clearly to remove the speck from your brother's eye. (Luke 6:41-42)

The Bible isn't a rulebook, and Christians cannot lift out of its context any passage from it, and still hope to gain a clear understanding of that passage.

It is important to understand that even the most fundamentalist Christian sects do not take the Bible wholly literally. The New Testament is two thousand years old, the old Testament much older. The Bible's cultural contexts, along with the translation at hand, is always taken into consideration by any Christian serious about understanding this vast and complex work.

To excerpt any isolated short passage from the Bible, and then claim for that passage absolute authority, is to fail to take the Bible on its own terms. If we wish to follow the word of God, then we must take the entirety of God's words into account. For example, when the Bible itself identifies some of its words as proverbs, it is bestowing upon those words less moral weight than other words that it identifies as commandments. The Bible itself tells us that some of its contents are songs, some visions, some histories, some dreams, some parables, and some commandments. The Bible itself also instructs Christians that New Testament moral directives super-sede Old Testament moral directives. The Bible itself tells us that its moral principles supersede any of its moral "rules."

The context of any Bible passage is as integral to its meaning as the passage itself. It may be appropriate to give equal weight to each clause within a business contract, each step within a set of mechanical instructions, or each rule within a game rulebook. But the Bible itself tells us that the Bible is not a uniform document, with each passage spelling out something clear and specific, and all passages having equal value. The Bible is not a *rulebook* for being Christian. We would be foolish to fail to understand that not everything in the Bible is a commandment, and that Christians cannot take a small section of the Bible out of its larger context, and still hope to gain a clear understanding of that section. Isolating a clobber passage from its context, and then claiming a sort of moral helplessness because "it's in the Bible," is failing to take the Bible either literally or seriously.

Using the four Old Testament passages to condemn all homo-sexual acts is not in keeping with any Christian directive from God, nor with the practices of contemporary Christians.

The Bible's first four references to homosexuality occur in the Old Testament.

While continuing to be spiritually inspired and influenced by the Old Testament, Christians were specifically instructed by Paul *not* to follow the law of the Old Testament, in such passages as:

The former regulation is set aside because it was weak and useless (for the law made nothing perfect), and a better hope is introduced, by which we draw near to God. (Hebrews 7:18-19)

Before the coming of this faith, we were held in custody under the law, locked up until the faith that was to come would be revealed. So the law was our guardian until Christ came that we might be justi-fied by faith. Now that this faith has come, we are no longer under a guardian. (Galatians 3:23-25)

So, my brothers and sisters, you also died to the law through the body of Christ, that you might belong to another ... (Romans 7:4)

For sin shall no longer be your master, because you are not under the law, but under grace. (Romans 6:14)

In practice, Christians do not follow the dictates of the Old Testament. If they did, polygamy would be legal, and things like tattoos, wearing mixed fabrics, eating pork, and seeding lawns with a variety of grasses would be forbidden. If Christians followed the dictates of the Old Testament, then today if the parents of a new bride could not, upon her husband's request, prove that she was a virgin, that bride would have to be stoned to death. Christians would also have to stone to death any Christian guilty of adultery. And the Christian day of worship would be Saturday, not Sunday.

Clearly, Christians no longer cleave to the rules of the Old Testament.

Therefore, the use of the four Old Testament passages to condemn all homosexual acts is not in keeping with any Christian directive from God, nor with the practices of contemporary Christians.

In the clobber passages Paul condemns the coercive, excessive, and predatory same-sex sexual activity practiced by the Romans—and would have condemned the same acts had they been heterosexual in nature.

Because Christians' understanding and practice of New Testament prescriptions naturally and inevitably evolve along with the society and culture of which they are a part, at any given time in history Christians have always *selectively* followed the dictates of the New Testament. Whenever a specific biblical injunction is found to be incongruous with contemporary mores, a reshaping of the conception of that injunction is not only widely accepted by Christians, it's encouraged, as long as the new thinking is understood to be in keeping with overriding timeless biblical moral principles. This is why Christian women no longer feel morally constrained to follow Paul's directives to leave their hair uncut, to keep their heads covered in church, or to always remain quiet in church. It's also why the Bible is no longer used to justify the cruel institution of slavery, or to deny women the right to vote.

Just as those thoughts and understandings of the New Testament changed and grew, so today is it becoming increasingly clear to Christians that the three New Testament clobber passages (each of which was written by Paul in letters to or about nascent distant churches), when understood in their historical context, do *not* constitute a directive from God against LGBT people today.

Here are the three references to homosexuality in the New Testament:

> Or do you not know that wrongdoers will not inherit the kingdom of God? Do not be deceived: Neither the sexually immoral nor idolaters nor adulterers nor men who have sex with men nor thieves nor the greedy nor drunkards nor slanderers nor swindlers will inherit the kingdom of God. (1 Corinthians 6:9-10)

> We also know that the law is made not for the righteous but for lawbreakers and rebels, the ungodly and sinful, the unholy and irreligious, for those who kill their fathers or mothers, for murderers, for the sexually immoral, for those practicing homosexuality, for slave traders and liars and perjurers—and for whatever else is contrary to the sound doctrine. (1 Timothy 1:9-10)

> Because of this, God gave them over to shameful lusts. Even their women exchanged natural sexual relations for unnatural ones. In the same way the men also abandoned natural relations with women and were inflamed with lust for one another. Men committed shameful acts with other men, and received in themselves the due penalty for their error. (Romans 1:26-27)

During the time in which the New Testament was written, the Roman conquerors of the region frequently and openly engaged in homosexual acts between themselves and boys. Such acts were also common between Roman men and their male slaves. These acts of *non-consensual* sex were considered normal and socially acceptable. They were, however, morally repulsive to Paul, as today they would be to everyone, gay and straight.

The universally acknowledged authoritative reference on matters of antiquity is the *Oxford Classical Dictionary*. Here is what the *OCD* (third edition revised, 2003) says in its section about homosexuality as practiced in the time of Paul:

> ... the sexual penetration of male prostitutes or slaves by conventionally masculine elite men, who might purchase slaves expressly for that purpose, was not considered morally problematic.

This is the societal context in which Paul wrote of homosexual acts, and it is this context that Christians must acknowledge when seeking to understand and interpret the three New Testament clobber passages. Yes, Paul condemned the same-sex sexual activity he saw around him—because it was coercive, without constraint, and between older men and boys. As a moral man, Paul was revolted by these acts, as, certainly, he would have been by the same acts had they been heterosexual in nature.

The Bible's clobber passages were written about same-sex acts between *heterosexual* persons, and do not address the subject of homosexual acts between a committed gay couple, because the concept of a person being homosexual did not exist at the time the Bible was written.

It is critical to our reading of the New Testament's three clobber passages to understand that while Paul would have known about sex acts that took place between persons of the same gender, he would have had no concept whatsoever of homosexual persons. Virtually no one in Paul's time was "out"; no one lived, or in any way publicly self-identified, as a homosexual. Paul had no reference point for an entire group of people who, as a fundamental, unalterable condition of their existence, were sexually attracted to persons of the same gender, and *not* sexually attracted to persons of the opposite gender.

Here is the opening of the *OCD*'s article on homosexuality:

> No Greek or Latin word corresponds to the modern term 'homosexuality,' and ancient Mediterranean society did not in practice treat homosexuality as a socially operating category of personal or public life. Sexual relations between persons of the same sex certainly did occur (they are widely attested in ancient sources), but they were not systematically distinguished or conceptualized as such, much less were they thought to represent a single, homogeneous phenomenon in contradistinction to sexual relations between persons of different sexes. ... The application of 'homosexuality' (and 'heterosexuality') in a substantive or normative sense to sexual expression in classical antiquity is not advised.

We can be confident that Paul was not writing to, or about, gay people, because he simply *could not have been,* any more than he could have written about smartphones, iPads, or televisions. We do not know what Paul might write or say today about gay people. All we know is that in the New Testament he wrote about promiscuous, predatory, non-consensual same-sex acts between people whom he understood to be heterosexual.

The Bible does condemn homosexual (and heterosexual) sex that is excessive, exploitive, and outside of marriage. It does *not,* however, address the state of homosexuality itself, much less the subject of homosexual acts between a married gay couple. Christians, therefore, have no Bible-based moral justification to condemn such acts.

Because there was no concept of gay marriage when the Bible was written, the Bible does not, and could not, address the sinfulness of homosexual acts *within* the context of gay marriage.

The Bible routinely, clearly, and strongly classifies all sex acts outside of the bonds of marriage as sinful. But, because when the Bible was written there was no concept of gay people—let alone, then, of gay marriage—the Bible does not, and could not, address the sinfulness of homosexual acts *within* the context of marriage.

By denying marriage equality to gay people, Christians are compelling gay couples to sin, because their intimacy must happen outside of marriage, and is therefore, by biblical definition, sinful. Christians, in other words, *cause* gay people to sin, and then blame the gay people for that sin. By any decent standard of morality that is manifestly and egregiously unfair.

Being personally repelled by homosexual sex doesn't make homosexual sex a sin.

In addition to the Bible, many Christians cite as evidence of the inherent sinfulness of homosexual acts their own emotional response to such acts. It is understandable that many straight people find homosexual sex repugnant (just as many gay people find heterosexual sex repugnant). It is normal for any one of us to be viscerally repelled by the idea of sex between, or with, people for whom we personally have no sexual attraction. Young people, for example, are often disgusted by the thought of senior citizens having sex. And who isn't repulsed by the idea of their own parents having sex? (When, rationally speaking, we should rejoice in the fact that they did—at least once!) But it is much too easy for any person to mistake their instinctive reaction against something as a moral reaction to that thing. Outrage isn't always *moral* outrage, though the two usually feel the same.

It may feel to a straight Christian that their instinctive negative reaction to homosexual sex arises from the Bible. But all of us necessarily view the Bible through the lens of our own experiences and prejudices, and we must be very careful to ensure that lens does not distort our reading of God's sacrosanct word.

"The greatest of these is love"

The overriding message of Jesus was love. Jesus modeled love, Jesus preached love, Jesus was love. Christians desiring to do and live the will of Jesus are morally obligated to always err on the side of love. Taken all together, the evidence—the social context in which the Bible was written, the lack of the very concept of gay people in Paul's time, the inability of gay people to marry, the inequity between how the clobber passages are applied between a majority and a minority population, the injustice of exclusion from both God's church on earth and human love generally as the punishment for a state of being over which one has no choice—conclusively shows that choosing to condemn and exclude gay people based on the Bible is the morally incorrect choice. That evidence should instead lead Christians to the most obvious, and most *Christian* of all positions, stated so beautifully by Paul himself in 1 Corinthians 13:8-13:

> Love never fails. But where there are prophecies, they will cease; where there are tongues, they will be stilled; where there is knowledge, it will pass away. For we know in part and we prophesy in part, but when completeness comes, what is in part disappears. When I was a child, I talked like a child, I thought like a child, I reasoned like a child. When I became a man, I put the ways of childhood behind me. For now we see only a reflection as in a mirror; then we shall see face to face. Now I know in part; then I shall know fully, even as I am fully known.

> And now these three remain: faith, hope and love. But the greatest of these is love.

Letters from Gay Christians

"I DID NOT WANT TO EXIST ANYMORE"

I was once a proud African Methodist Episcopal Zion (AME Zion) Christian, the evangelical son of an AME Zion preacher, ready to answer the call of a life in ministry. Once I claimed the faith of my father as my own, I felt a denominational identity was too constricting. I simply called myself an evangelical Christian. This, despite the fact that I was tremendously hurt and confused by the near daily abuse I suffered at the hands of Christian school classmates, who taunted me with "faggot," "girly," "gay-gay," etc.

Clearly, everyone else had figured out my sexual orientation before I had. When I thought about the fact that, unlike my 13-year-old counterparts, I didn't seem to be interested in girls, that in fact I longed to be close to and have sex with boys, I immediately reasoned, "But I can't be gay, because Christians aren't gay, and I'm a Christian!"

It was just a phase. I couldn't be gay.

This "phase" lasted several years (despite desperate pleas to an almighty God who would no doubt free me of this "sin" that I wanted no part of anymore than He did). After struggling with a four-year addiction to gay porn, in my senior year of college I was forced to acknowledge that this must be more than a mere phase. I did what any good evangelical Christian would: I sought help. After a night of binging on porn, I tapped out the words "gay and Christian" on the keyboard, and came across Exodus International, a ministry dedicated to helping men and women overcome "unwanted same-sex attractions."

Initially, discovering Exodus gave me hope and encouragement. I went along under the notion that this was no phase, but that it was manageable and conquerable. I dove into ministry: Bible study founder/leader in college, president of the Christian group at pharmacy school, volunteering with the youth ministry at my local Assembly of God church.

Yet the more I explored my sexual attractions, the more dismayed I became. I fervently desired a Godly relationship with a woman, to be a dad; I yearned to live the evangelical, American dream.

What I could not shake, though, was the debilitating loneliness that overshadowed every aspect of my life—despite a loving family, a wonderful girlfriend, a supportive ex-gay community, an adept counselor, great accountability partners, service to others, leadership in ministry, a local church community, incessant prayer, indomitable determination, and innumerable ex-gay resources. As I became increasingly aware of my unchanging orientation, the insufficient satisfaction of opposite gender intimacy, and the idea that this meant a lifetime of misery without true companionship, my depression and anxiety grew, until I was ready for God to just take me home.

I simply did not want to exist anymore, and begged God to have mercy on me by ending this.

I wish I could say that my Christian community responded in Christ-like ways to me when I revealed my "struggles with same-sex attraction." And there surely were those who incarnated Christ to me. But more commonly the responses ranged from indifference to muted disgust (and everything in between).

In one pivotal encounter, I had lunch with the youth pastor at my Assembly of God church. I was sharing with him my disappointment with the way in which my revelation was received by the other young adults in the church with whom I was desperate to bond (after all, the ex-gay mantra was that "healing comes by forging healthy, same-sex relationships"). I bemoaned the fact that some of those in whom I had confided were nonplussed, some cool but silent (leaving me to wonder where I actually stood with them), and yet others took it upon themselves to preach to me, thinking that an "encouragement."

What was my pastor's response to my discouragement? He spent ninety minutes chiding me for being upset, and preaching to me about the evils of homosexuality. The obvious offense (treating me in a manner expressly as I had just complained about being treated by others) was only magnified by the fact that he was well aware of my dad's ordination in ministry, my years spent in Bible classes at Christian schools, and my extensive knowledge of scripture. Perhaps most damaging of all was his insistence that I no longer serve with our church youth group (which he had originally mandated prior to our lunch date). I cannot express how belittled and useless I felt. My love for God, my gifts, my talents counted for naught so long as I had difficulties dealing with my sexuality. I left lunch that day feeling more disparaged than when we started.

I was never an evangelical after that. In fact, here I stand, six years later, and there are times when it is difficult for me to associate myself with Christianity at all. After hearing my protracted story, religious and irreligious people alike often ask me in befuddled exasperation: "How are you still a Christian? Why do you still go to church?!" And frankly, I have yet to articulate a satisfactory answer. As best I can tell, though, it is rooted in my abiding love for Jesus. I am compelled by the life and teachings of Jesus. I strive to live The Way of Jesus, and to bring the Kingdom of Peace and Love here to earth. And yet every day it is a struggle to hold onto that shred of faith, when so many other self-proclaimed Christians adamantly declare my apostasy and condemnation to hell for daring to love in the way that comes naturally to me. (The more enlightened folks are civil enough to quietly suggest I'm "not in God's will," and to let me know that they are praying for me to see the light and truly know Him.)

I profusely thank God for the emerging church I discovered around the time of that fateful lunch with my pastor. Up until that point, I had a subtle but nagging twist in my gut at every church I had ever attended. It was from experiencing such love and comfort at this new church that I was finally able to verbalize what I felt all those years: that I was not safe and accepted as I was. At last, I was blessed to have been led to a community of believers who would walk alongside me, instead of ahead of me; who would ask questions with me, instead of dictating beliefs to me. It was within this community that I was able to salve the wounds of bitterness and jadedness that had pervaded my soul.

I don't know that I'll ever be an evangelical again. I'm not sure if I can even maintain the identity "Christian," given all the baggage that seems to accompany the word. All I know is that I hope for the day when I can be seen by the Church as being equal to all others in the Body of Christ, and worthy of sharing my gifts in faithful service—not despite my sexuality, but because *I am a gay Christian,* beloved of God.

— D.J.F., MARYLAND

"IS MY PRETENSE WORTH IT?"

In high school, I was secretary of our newly formed Bible club. Every Wednesday I would wake up at five a.m. in order to get to the school by six, so that the club could meet before class started. I was already the odd one out for being the only Catholic in this group of born-again Christians, so I always felt this weird drive to try and fit in with the rest of the club.

One day the teacher who led the group announced that we were going to do a special project: write letters to a gay group informing them that being gay was a sin.

I was thunderstruck. How did my innocent little school group go from Bible study and Bible Pictionary to political activism (that it was presumed we all agreed with)? My classmates hopped to it: to my eyes there wasn't one who hesitated. If I said I didn't want to write such a letter, I felt certain they would all pounce on me with Leviticus lectures, as surely as if I had marched in there waiving a rainbow flag and then kissed another girl.

I should mention that at this point in my life, I was so blinded by "Christian" dogma that I couldn't even admit to myself that I was gay. I was repulsed by boys, confounded by my boy-crazy gal pals, and cried the first time a boy tried to kiss me. But I was Christian, so couldn't *possibly* be gay! So it wasn't for myself (at least consciously) that I was hesitant to write the letters. My hesitation was based on the moral principle informing the project; I didn't agree with its overall assertion. It was also based on my one bisexual friend, whom I knew to be a good person; it didn't seem to me that she was inherently a sinner just because she liked women as well as men.

However, with everyone diligently writing away, and the teacher noticing my lack of participation, I caved. I did not want to be the freak show in this group any more than I already was. I did not want to be singled out.

My letter said something about how the only time *anybody* is supposed to have sex is if they are married and actively trying to make babies—which meant that not only priests, but any unmarried Christian person was therefore called to chastity. So, I argued, it's not gay love that's the problem, since Jesus taught love, but just the *sex*, which is a problem for everyone.

Shame-faced, I gave the teacher my letter. He was "approving" them before sending them off to whatever unfortunate group received them. It turns out I was singled out after all—for, in his words, writing the most thoughtful and well-argued letter of the bunch. I was praised for how well I had betrayed my own ethics.

I remember wishing that whatever group got those letters would just toss them unread into a fireplace.

It wasn't until years later that I was able to admit to myself that I was gay—and that was the happiest, most liberating experience I've ever had. Of course, I had years before then left any form of Christian church. Now I've been testing the waters on an attempted return back, secure enough in who I am to not let those same negative attitudes that drove me away the first time cause me to lie to myself any longer. But it still hurts to know that I will never be fully accepted for who I am by those I would like to call "family"—that is, a church family. Other members can talk about their significant others, their kids, their weddings, their anniversaries. When they do I smile and nod, the same as I did in my high school Bible club, and let them tell me with condescending smiles not to worry, that one day I'll find Mr. Right.

Is it worth it to have the peace that church brings me, if that peace is counteracted by the play-acting I have to undertake in order to be welcome there?

— W.P., DENVER, COLORADO

"AN ACHING LONELINESS"

As the oldest son of Pentecostal pastors who founded eleven churches throughout Australia, the church was the closest thing to a home I ever knew. My first memory was crawling on the floor of a meeting hall during a worship service while my mother played the piano and my father exhorted the congregation to engage in the Pentecostal two-step. It was only natural that I grew up expecting to be a pastor myself.

As a small child I would take my teddy bears on imaginary adventures down the Amazon River. Inevitably (after numerous interruptions, such as wrestling crocodiles or surviving typhoons), I would assemble my teddies for an alter call. After all, one never knew when they were going to be carried off to the great big stuffing centre in the sky.

As the oldest son, I considered it my duty to look after the other kids at church. When I was young, I'd make sure that all the kids had things like proper lunch invitations; later, I took on overseeing our church's children and youth group ministries. Growing up, there seemed to me no higher calling than being part of building the church of God.

Everything changed when I was about fifteen years old. Everyone else seemed to be experiencing these powerful urges and desires, while I felt like a disinterested bystander. It's not that I experienced "gay" thoughts. I had no framework for what I was feeling at all, other than deep dread. So I adopted the most reasonable Anglo-Saxon response, and repressed every shred of emotional attachment to men that I experienced.

In addition to dissembling from myself, I developed a mental warning system to ensure that others never came to suspect there was something deeply wrong with me. Before talking, I would mentally review what I was about to say, to ensure that it fit within an 'approved' social construct. Dull. People could intuitively tell that I was holding back and not relaxing around them, and the strain of maintaining this role meant that there was no capacity to develop real friendships.

With a deep and abiding sense that something was wrong with me, I never pursued my involvement with the church. That was until my late twenties. Despite the beginnings of a successful career as an economist, I left the Reserve Bank of Australia to study theology. My primary motivation was to try and change myself so that I could have what my social circle considered a proper relationship. But so much of my energy was focused on maintaining the appropriate social facade there was very little behind the image to give to another human being.

Long story short: God didn't change me. Not for a lack of trying on my part. I spent so many nights crying myself to sleep because of an aching loneliness.

After fifteen years, everything changed for me when a friend pushed me to consider that I could be gay and *Christian*. This was a truly radical thought. Through exploring it I was able to come to terms with my sexuality: I realized that, without any conscious volitional control, my heart would fall in love with men.

Why worship a God of love if doing so means denying the possibility of experiencing love?

From the point that I accepted my own ability to love, and to receive love, everything in my life changed. I have met, and married (to the limits of the law) my life partner. We've been together for over six years. And in that time I can unequivocally say that I've become a much better person. I've become a much better Christian.

I now walk closer to God than ever before. I don't know if I will ever get to heaven, but I certainly know life on earth is no longer a hell I need to escape. I love my life, and the people in it, far more now than I ever could before.

— N.T., Australia

"A BETTER WORLD IF I WAS DEAD"

I was four years old when I decided that I believed what my parents had told me about Jesus. Ever since that day I've tried to become more and more like Him, and tried to learn about who God is. I go on mission trips, I teach children's Sunday School, I don't drink or smoke, I read my Bible. I pray daily for the healing of our world. After I graduate from college this year, I plan to go to divinity school so I can better serve others with Christ's love.

I'm also gay. I was raised a Southern Baptist from the day I was born. I was home-schooled, and never took a single class at a public school, so I wasn't "indoctrinated." I didn't know anyone who was gay; I didn't even know that such a thing existed until I was probably eleven or twelve. I have always had wonderful, warm, close relationships with both my parents and my younger brother. I've always considered myself a political moderate who leans toward libertarianism, so I never felt much if any attraction toward standard liberal political positions. I have never experienced abuse of any kind. No explanation exists that can explain what "made" me gay. I certainly didn't choose it.

When I realized that I wasn't straight—and "wasn't straight" became clear to me long before the "is gay" part did—every single person I knew at the time was deeply opposed to any kind of acceptance of gay people. When I realized what was going on with me, I was terrified. Night after night I prayed for God to change it, to make me the person that everyone had always told me I would be. Then, typically, I would cry myself to sleep. Was the problem with me that I didn't have enough faith? I wondered. I read my Bible more, and spent time on the websites of groups like Exodus International and others who said they could make me straight. Nothing worked.

I stopped trying to change who I was when I was fourteen, but that didn't really fix things either; it just made it a little easier to breathe. But once I admitted to myself that it was true that I'm gay, a sense of real dread set in. It could never be good, I knew. The best case scenario for my life could never be good. I couldn't do the things that would bring my life meaning. I wanted love and a family. I've always really, really wanted to join the Air Force. But most of all, I just wanted to be able to stop lying all the time, and I really couldn't do that, either.

For over a year, I was deeply suicidal. I think people assume that being suicidal is a moment, an instant, an event that happens and is then either beaten or given into. For me at least, it's never been that way. It's the exhausting grind of living every day wanting nothing more than for the pain to stop, praying every night that you won't wake up, and starting every morning disappointed. I've stood in the shower staring at my razor more times than I can count. I've thought endlessly about how people might react to my suicide, what would happen after I did it. I've scratched my arms raw and dug my fingernails into my palms so hard that I bled, all in an attempt to stop feeling like dying was the best option for me. Better to die now, while things are at least okay. Better to let them remember me like this. Once everyone finds out I'm gay, my life may as well be over. Better for them never to find out. And if this really is who I am—and I knew it was—then there's only one way for that to happen.

That was my thinking at fifteen years old. Feeling like I would be completely hated and unwanted by the people I loved was unbearable. Every time I heard them make a snide comment about Ellen

DeGeneres or *Brokeback Mountain,* it was like a physical blow. Every time they said God had abandoned America because America was supposedly too accepting of "the homosexual agenda," all I wanted was to curl up and die. Assuming that theft, lying, and other sins don't happen at lower rates among gay people than straight ones, it logically follows that Christians who think homosexuality is a sin also think gay people, as a group, are less moral than straight people. So according to that simple logic, the world would be a more moral place, on average, if all we gay people were dead. Or gone. Or whatever. But a world without gay people would be ideal.

My life was already painful enough at fifteen. At that point my life was no fun at all; it wasn't even tolerable. How big a step is it from "The world would be a more moral, and therefore better, place, if there were no gay people in it," to, "The world generally, and I personally, will be better off if I was dead"?

I'm lucky, because I got some amazing therapy, and found a church that loves me. I've come to realize that God's love is broader than my mind can imagine, and that my only purpose here on this earth is to love God with all my heart, and to love my neighbor as myself. I've dedicated my life to the church, I deeply believe in the importance of families, and as cheesy as it might sound, I love Jesus. I'm really not that scary, I don't think. I'm actually probably a little bit boring. I'm just grateful that God chose to put treasure in earthen vessels, instead of only using people whose journeys have been smooth and easy. May the peace of Christ be with you, and his presence your guide.

— K.J., NORTH CAROLINA

"I WAS IN UNSAFE TERRITORY"

I have known since third or fourth grade that I was gay. All the other girls in my class had a huge crush on the new boy, Cameron, while I was crushing on my best friend. Even then I knew, somehow, that whatever was different about me wasn't just different, but wrong. I never told anyone about being attracted to the other girls in my class, the crushes on my female teachers, or my complete lack of attraction to guys. I learned to fake normal, so that no one would think anything was wrong with me. My family was involved in an ultra-conservative fundamentalist Christian church, so it was easy to pass off my lack of a dating life by saying "my family won't allow me to date non-Christians," or some other such nonsense. All the while I kept my attraction to women deeply hidden, terrified of what would happen if anyone in my family or church found out.

When I was a senior in high school, a girl from my youth group admitted to me that she was gay. Rather than rallying around her, or providing her the love and support that she surely needed in this time of vulnerability, I joined the rest of my youth group in shunning her. At the direction of our youth pastor, we did not invite this girl to any social events, or include her in our circles anymore. Needless to say, she quit attending church soon after that. I am not proud of what I did to my friend, but that event certainly did reinforce to me the necessity of keeping my secret deep in the closet.

After graduating high school I attended a strict fundamentalist Christian university, where I was placed in an all-girls dorm, surrounded by girls who were at college to get a "Mrs." degree. I hated being in the dorm, listening to the endless talk of which boy was most desirable, and who was dating whom. I hated it because I didn't understand it, and because I could never, ever tell anyone about the cute girl two doors down, or the girl who sat next to me in freshman English. Surrounded by people, I felt more alone than ever. Add to this the rumors that occasionally circulated about girls who were found kissing in closets and were immediately sent packing, and I knew I was in unsafe territory.

All this time I never prayed about my homosexuality. I knew God loved me, and I loved Him, but it was almost as if I felt like that love would disappear if He discovered my secret. I kept hoping that I would study enough, or learn enough, or serve enough to finally find that secret formula that would make me like everyone else.

One day in graduate school (at the same fundamentalist Christian university) I was in chapel, where I heard delivered a strong anti-homosexuality message. The preacher basically said, "If you are even slightly tempted by same-sex desires, then you are in sin and need to get help." He mentioned a couple of ex-gay ministries that are committed to helping people recover from homosexuality.

As I sat and listened, I was terrified. What if someone had found out about me? Did this mean that God hated me? Did I really have some big scary sin problem that needed to be solved? After much time spent praying and crying and begging God for this not to be true, I decided to get some help.

Unfortunately, my pastor's wife had not been trained to deal with recovering homosexuals, so she was able to offer little help. She suggested that I tell a couple of close friends, so that they could pray for me and keep me accountable for my sin issues. Not knowing what else to do, and desperate to solve this horrible problem in my life (and terrified that my sin problem would make me ineligible for serving God), I followed her instructions to the letter.

Coming out to my Christian friends turned out to be the biggest disaster of my life. Each time I told them something along the lines of, "I have a sin problem. I am struggling with homosexuality. I know it is wrong, and I don't want to be this way, and I am getting help. Will you please pray for me?" And each time the friend would panic and abandon me. A couple of my friends told me they had spoken with their parents about me, and had been advised not to be friends with me anymore. Others said that we could still be friends, but that we would now have rules to follow, such as keeping open our dorm room doors when we were visiting each other, or not eating together in the cafeteria. Some pushed notes under my dorm room door telling me that they couldn't or wouldn't talk to me anymore.

My best friend just said, "Why are you telling me this?" and left me. She never explained why she disappeared, but every time I called to see if we could do dinner or something, she always had other plans.

So there I was, struggling with what I thought was the biggest, worst sin issue in the world, and my support network had utterly fallen away from me.

At that point I determined that I would continue to fight this sin of homosexuality, but that I wouldn't tell anyone else about it anymore. I retreated deeper into the closet, only emerging online, where I was involved in several ex-gay chat rooms and forums. I started praying that God would take this horrible affliction away from me. I begged God; I promised Him everything in the world, all the while trying my hardest to like guys, and *not* to like girls.

Nothing helped. I just became more and more frustrated. Meanwhile, my straight Christian friends (who thought I was a straight Christian) were dating, getting married, and having children, while all I could picture for myself was a lifetime of hiding and hurting.

After six years attending a fundamentalist Christian college, and six years teaching in a private Christian school in Guam, all the while hoping that all of this ministry surrounding me would cure me, I finally left the ministry. I was burned out as a teacher; I had decided that I no longer agreed with a lot of the teachings of the fundamentalist church I was required to attend; and I was ready to be an adult and make my own adult decisions. I returned to the States, moving in with family in the San Francisco Bay Area. I wasn't sure what I believed anymore, or what was important, but I knew I needed some time to recover and refocus.

Contrary to the fears of my fundamentalist friends, I did not shave my head, get a bunch of tattoos, or take up smoking. But I did start attending a non-denominational church, reading the Bible, and thinking for myself. Not only that, but being in the Bay Area exposed me to lots of different kinds of people with lots of different beliefs. The West Coast really was an ideal location for me, since everyone there seemed to be pretty accepting of others' beliefs, and very open to new and different ideas. For the first time I was able to toy with the idea that maybe, just maybe, homosexuality wasn't a disease to be cured. Maybe it was okay to be gay and Christian. Maybe God could still love me.

I quit visiting the ex-gay online chat rooms, and instead started studying what "the other side" thought about homosexuality. And I discovered that there are a lot of people, even Christian people, who think that homosexuality is something you are born with, and that it cannot be changed through therapy or treatment. I even found Christians who advocated gay marriage. The tension that had built up in my body over the past years began to roll off me, and I could feel my muscles relaxing. For the first time ever I could imagine myself finding that special someone and dating her. I could imagine myself part of a family. I could imagine myself loving and being loved.

The future seemed so much brighter and hopeful. I began to look forward to the next days and weeks and months to see what they would bring.

My faith is very important to me. My orientation is, too, and it wasn't until recently that I was able to allow the two to coexist peacefully. I was reading in Matthew 8, where Jesus heals a man who has leprosy. The first three verses of that story say, "When Jesus came down from the mountainside, large crowds followed him. A man with leprosy came and knelt before him and said, 'Lord, if you are willing, you can make me clean.' Jesus reached out his hand and touched the man. 'I am willing,' he said. 'Be clean!'"

I cannot even begin to count the number of times that I have prayed, "Lord, if you are willing, you can make me straight." Always before, God was silent on the issue. For the first time ever, I finally heard Him speak. He said, "My precious child, you are not sick. I don't fix what isn't broken. I love you just as you are."

If I could say anything to evangelical Christians, I would ask them to do two things. First, please consider the people Jesus spent time around and the people He condemned. He spent time with the outcasts of society, those who were left out and not accepted by the rest of society. He never carried a sign or shouted hateful words. His condemnation was reserved for those who were so proud that they prevented others from coming to Him. His anger was directed at those who crossed off His "whosoever," and posted a list of acceptable people. For the rest of the world, He had nothing but compassion and mercy. I am afraid that the church has missed its opportunity to share Jesus' love with the hurting members of the LGBT community. Too many people have been turned off to church and to God because of the hatred spewed at them for who they are.

The second thing I would ask is for evangelical Christians to educate themselves, and consider other perspectives. Homosexuality is not a choice. (Do you really think I would have *chosen* to be this way, to have to deal with all this difficulty and pain?) You cannot get HIV from hugging a gay person. Please, please combat your ignorance with some education. If you don't know much about LGBT people, get to know some. Spend time with them. Love them the way Christ does. You'll accomplish two things with this: you will expand your own horizons—your own ministry—and you will allow another human being to see God's love. Because that's the crux of the issue: the church is teaching LGBT people that God hates them, when the same Christ who died on the cross for straight people also died for the LGBT community. Don't nullify Christ's work with your own hate and ignorance.

— J.F., SAN FRANCISCO, CALIFORNIA

"MY SON AND I AREN'T WELCOMED"

I am a Christian and I am a lesbian. I was created by God just like everyone else. I live with these two labels as one. They are both woven into the fabric of my being.

I have had my share of adversity in life. Growing up in an affluent family, I hid my suffering of sexual and physical abuse. I endured things that no child should ever have to.

As an adult I tried to conform to what was then accepted by society, and I married a man. I loved him with everything I had, and had a child with him, even though my heart knew that I was lying to myself. I was born gay and was compelled to unhappily conform to the norm. I stayed with my husband for seven years, and tried to make it work. While I did love him as a person, we never had that husband/wife connection, even though I tried so hard to find it. I wanted to be like everyone else—but I wasn't. God did not create me that way.

After seven years of trying to make my hetero marriage work, I left my husband. I didn't leave him in order to pursue a lesbian relationship, but rather because he began using drugs, and became extremely violent. I left to protect my child.

I know that some people have theories that types of abuse can "turn people gay," but it is quite the opposite. It was first growing up in an abusive family, and then being in an abusive marriage, that held me so tightly in denial. I completely lost who I was, because I lived in such fear. When I got out of my abusive environment—and when I worked hard in therapy for two years—I finally began to find myself. I realized that it's okay to be me.

Today I'm an award-winning teacher, an artist, a mother, a strong woman, a fighter, a community leader, a Christian, and a lesbian.

When I look back on the abuse and hard times I've suffered, I know there was one common presence that was always there pulling me through: my faith. God was always with me. He was there when I was that hurt little girl being sexually abused. He was there when my life was in danger from my husband. He was there when I had to make the decision to escape domestic violence. He was there when I had the courage to come out and be who I really am. God will always be there for me, as He has always been.

I have been asked by people questioning my faith: "If God was present when all of those bad things were happening to you, why didn't He protect you?" My answer is always that He did. Without God, I would have never survived. Without God, I would not have the will to keep going. Without God, I would not have hope for a better future for my son. I know God, who is in my heart, loves me for who I am.

I have taught my son Christian values and the principles of love and acceptance. I teach him that God is love, and that *everyone* is created in His image. I also teach him that God is in one's heart, not just in a book or church building. Unfortunately, with some of the hatred found in churches, he and I are not welcomed in most churches. I often wonder if God is sad when He sees His name being used as a justification for hate and exclusion.

There have been times when I have really struggled and cried over this. It hurts me to know that so many "religious leaders" and "followers of Christ" choose to follow instead the path of fear and hate. The popular phrase "What would Jesus do?" so often comes to my mind. I know without a doubt that Jesus would treat us all the same, and welcome us into His church and into His arms. That's why my sadness never lingers. My faith is in God, and not in humanity. Humans make mistakes—but God did not make a mistake when He made me as He did. It is my hope that one day the Christian church will open its heart to everyone.

— L.T., SOUTH CAROLINA

"I WAS SCARED"

I am Catholic. And I am gay. I went to Catholic grade school, with the disgusting Catholic school uniforms and the strict, old-timer priest. I hated it, because we learned about all the things that would land us in hell (i.e., getting divorced, masturbating, *being gay*). I then went to a Catholic high school—which, being a high school, was a bit less conservative. Still, I was a closeted gay teenager at a religious institution.

For my freshman and sophomore years at that school, I didn't even think about telling people about my sexuality. Looking back, I guess the religion thing did have something to do with that. I was scared that if I told one person, they would tell people, and then the whole school would know—and before long so would the school's administration. Not okay. It wasn't until the middle of my junior year that I decided to open up a bit, and come out to one friend. Then two. Then a whole group of friends I trusted. And everything was okay. I felt safe at my school, even though only a small number of people knew who I really was.

Then came senior year. And if learning religion up to that point had meant learning what would get you into hell, in senior year we learned the opposite. We learned about Jesus' love for us. As a senior I was selected to become a member of the Campus Ministry's retreat team, leading the underclassmen on their retreats in the woods. It was fun, teaching the younger kids about how much Jesus loves us. I would always say those things, but I never really understood them until the time came for the special senior retreat. It was the mother of all spiritual retreats. Four days out in the wilderness, put into groups of kids you don't really know.

On the third night of the retreat I opened myself up to the eight individuals in my group, people to whom I'd never really spoken, but only glanced at in the hallways at school. It was amazing. They showed me support, compassion, friendship, understanding, and *love.*

My experience up in the mountains was so amazing that I signed up for (and was selected to be) a leader for the next retreat. But then I realized something: as a leader, you are required to give a speech to the entire retreat group (usually around sixty-plus people). In this speech, leaders usually reveal something significant about themselves. In thinking about the speech I would give, I thought, "Man, my life is pretty damn boring—except for that one little detail ..."

During the six weeks of preparation before the retreat, I debated with myself over whether or not I should come out during my speech. I consulted my friends, my retreat group, and even the other students that were leading with me. And they all said the same thing: "Do it, but only if you feel comfortable." And I figured, what the hell? I'm comfortable. And so, after weeks of preparing my speech, the four-day retreat came. I learned that my talk wasn't until the very *end* of the four days, however. So on each day of the retreat my stomach kept filling with more and more nerves. The night before my talk, after my group of kids opened their hearts out to me, I went back to my room and almost threw up. I thought, "What am I doing? I can't go up there and say that!" Because for me, coming out to that group of over sixty people meant that it would be over. I would lose control of who knew what at school. This wouldn't be kept on the retreat. Rumors would be spread. And faculty members would find out. Granted, I would be graduating from my high school in a couple months, but still.

The Fourth Day came. I got ready for my talk. Before I spoke, as per the tradition, all of the fellow leaders prayed over me. As one of my fellow leaders lead the prayer over me I completely lost it. I began bawling. And I hadn't even started yet. This was going to be tough. I was able to calm down and catch myself before I started. My speech began well, with a couple of jokes thrown in—and then I got into the serious stuff. The theme of my talk was basically about how to be a good person. As an example of when I *had* been a good person, I gave a real (and emotional) story of a time when I had been a good person by helping a friend out of depression.

As an example of how in some ways I didn't feel like a good person, I discussed how I was somewhat disconnected from my family, how I didn't let them into my life like I should.

"And most importantly," I said, "they don't know that I'm gay."

Bam. There it was. I'd said it.

I looked around the room to see people's reactions. Blank stares, or so it seemed. I had more, so I kept reading. I gave a brief recollection of how I used to be scared because I was different, but how I wasn't scared anymore. (I looked around again, and saw some people crying. I was still dry-eyed). Then I went back to my family, talking about how all I wanted from them was acceptance, but that I didn't feel like I could ever tell them about me. (More people crying; I'm still dry-eyed). All I wanted, I said, was to tell my family that I loved them. (Entire room crying; I'm still dry-eyed).

When my speech was over I went to go sit in the back of the crowded room with the rest of the leaders. I still had not cried. One of the adult leaders, a teacher, came over to me from the other side of the room. She was crying. I stood up to give her a hug, and once we made contact I lost it. I don't think I have ever cried that hard. When she let go, I found that the other leaders (both adult and student) were waiting to give me a hug. With each hug they whispered to me words of support and love.

One of the adult leaders was a priest. He too came and gave me a hug, and I'll never forget his words to me. "You are a courageous person," he said. "You are a happy person. You are a good person."

Once all the leaders had hugged me, I sat back down and regained myself. Then came the kids on the retreat. Damn—I lost it once more. Every single retreat member waited in line to come and give me his or her love and support. I had never in my life felt so accepted and loved. And through all of this I knew, too, that Jesus loved me.

The retreat ended, and it was back to school on Monday. But now it was different. I walked around school looking at how many people knew I was gay. And everything was fine. It was amazing. A couple of weeks later I started hearing that people were talking about it. The rumors were spreading. My entire class basically knew. And no one said anything to me about it. No one ever gave me trouble. It was weird at first, but it turned out better than okay. It was great. We graduated and moved on and that's it. Everything was fine, and I realized that I had no reason to be scared just because of the school's religious affiliation. If anything, the religious affiliation made it possible for me to be as open as I am today. I was even able to come out to my father before graduation. Now I am waiting to begin my freshmen year of college. I'm ready to move out and start a new life in a new city, all while remembering that Jesus is with me in my heart forever.

— M.O., CALIFORNIA

"I LIVED IN TERROR"

At a conservative church campground near my house, I was walking around with two of my favorite cousins during a huge family reunion. It was lunchtime, and masses of unfamiliar relatives swarmed the lunch bar.

Of my two companions, Shirley was nearest my age. She and I were so strongly bonded that her mom (my aunt) always joked about being afraid that she and I would move to Utah together to get married. I only saw Shirley once or twice a year because she lived quite far away, but whenever together we were inseparable.

With the two of us was Nancy, my older cousin. I always looked up to Nancy, the epitome of a righteous young Christian woman. Her family was much more conservative than mine, and she was one of the kindest people I knew. Nancy respected her parents, told the truth when it was hard, and treated me with kindness even when I sometimes didn't deserve it.

Pointing to a woman in line at the lunch bar, Nancy said, "We can't sit by her."

"Why?" I asked.

"Because she's gay."

"What does that mean?"

"It means she likes women."

"So what?"

"She likes women the way *men* are supposed to like women. And the Bible says you can't sit at the table with that kind of person."

As an adult I now know that this theological stance is taken from 1 Cor. 5:11: "But now I am writing you that you must not associate with anyone who calls himself a brother but is sexually immoral or greedy, an idolater or a slanderer, a drunkard or a swindler. With such a man do not even eat."

Interestingly, I've never seen this verse applied toward anyone *but* homosexuals—who are not specifically mentioned at all.

To this day I love Nancy, and respect the dedication that she shows in her Christian walk. I've never told her that I am a homosexual, or what a horrible shadow her words cast over my childhood and adolescence. I come from a very strong Christian background. Both of my parents are Mennonite, a denomination that has primarily grown through the bearing of children. My paternal grandfather is one of ten children, and two of my mom's sisters have seven kids.

When I realized that I was "a gay," I closed the closet door hard, and lived in terror that some day my family would discover my secret, and that I would then be cut off from everyone and everything I knew and loved. Some may not understand this, but if you knew that ninety percent of my friends were relatives, and that I was related to everyone in my church youth group and nearly a third of those in my public school class, you might understand what a huge part of my world was threatened.

Not to mention that I was already seriously, passionately in love with Jesus Christ. Every day that I felt attraction towards a man I hated myself, detested the fact that I was a man, and begged Jesus to make it all go away. I prayed often for forgiveness and change, but things never got better. When I discovered pornography, they got worse. I was a slave to pornography for a long time, and still have problems with it. I was too scared to get help.

My parents finally found some pictures on my computer when I was a senior in high school. They cried, and the next day called our pastor to the house. I was so humiliated, but at the same time felt a huge weight lifted from my shoulders. At least I didn't have to carry the secret alone anymore.

Our pastor prayed with us, and questioned me, finding that my theology was sound and proper. (I believed that homosexuality was wrong, even though I was powerless to change it within myself.) He anointed me with oil (though he made sure to let me know that God rarely chose to heal immediately). My parents discussed counseling with me, but the nearest counselor with any experience with "that problem" was almost three hours away, and I didn't think I could bring myself to drive there by myself. Plus, I was already eighteen, and about to head off for college.

Freshman year at a state university was interesting. I had come out to some of my youth group over the summer, and at university I came out to some more people: a few Christian friends, a lesbian friend, a gay friend, and my roommates. My roommates were pretty nonchalant about it, but (strangely enough) my lesbian friend kept trying to "convert" me.

I went to a secular counselor at the university in hopes of changing my orientation, but he offered no help beyond a seminar on reconciling Christianity and homosexuality. As a conservative, I assumed all such theology was a sham, that homosexuals and liberal Christians twisted the Bible to excuse their behaviors.

The following year I transferred to a small Bible junior college. A friend there convinced me of the constitutional rights of gays to get married. I came out to a few of my friends there. So far I had experienced no rejection in my coming out (though I can hardly call it coming out; it was more like confession).

After receiving my associate degree in Biblical Studies, I was called to go on a mission trip. I spent three months in training with thirty people in a three-story house in Columbus, Ohio. Every Friday we gave our "pilgrimages," a fifteen minute recounting of our lives or spiritual journeys. There was a lot of heavy stuff. I told everyone of my struggles. As part of my application I had already informed the program director of my particular struggle.

The training was incredible, and through it I felt closer to God than I have ever felt in my life. Amazing things happened as we had speakers come in and tell us about things happening around the world, about the movement of the Kingdom of God. We experienced and practiced prophesy, healing, and awesome prayer times with God.

I was subsequently in Asia for six months. My time there was less exciting than my training had been. My team was in a restricted country, and we couldn't talk about Jesus very openly. There were no conversions, and I left feeling that we had accomplished nothing substantial. I had also expected that during the course of the mission, I would be healed of my homosexuality. But I wasn't.

I came home and spent a wonderful summer working with my family on our farm. I then enrolled in a Christian university, where I made some more wonderful friends. During that college's orientation week I told a friend about my "struggles," and found that he was the same as me. After a really long conversation about it, we prayed; afterwards, he said we probably shouldn't ever again be alone together. After that he hardly ever spoke to me at all.

I didn't come out to anyone else at that school, though I now wish I had. One of my close friends from those days has since told me that he never thought homosexuality was wrong—and I think at the time he knew I was gay. But coming out to him or anyone else frightened me, because I was afraid I would "stray" from the righteous path of repression if I had the freedom that comes with letting people know who you really are. I had already become so much more liberal through my discussions at Bible college and during the missions program. So now I chose to close down again, and for a year and a half became less open than I had been.

I graduated in December, 2010, and now live in Columbus, Ohio. Over the past couple of months, I have come to the point where I believe that God made me the way I am: that he loves me, and that it is possible for me to be both gay and Christian.

When I look at the Church, and then toward the gay community, my heart hurts. So many gay people seem to grow up in Christian homes. So many *would* love Christ, but have learned to hate the church for what it has done, and continues to do, to them.

Besides the sexually immoral, mentioned in the verse I cited above are greedy people, idolaters, slanderers, drunkards, and swindlers. Of all those sorts of people, the only ones not welcomed in most churches are the "sexually immoral"—which is somehow *always* taken to mean gays. No church holds rallies to legislate against any of those other sorts of persons; they don't take up picket signs damning idolaters or slanderers to hell.

My vision of the church is a place where all people who love Jesus are comfortable, and those who don't know him are welcomed. I was really excited to see church booths at Pridefest. It was my first time going to such an event, and as I walked past one of the church booths I heard a Pride participant say, "There's a *Jesus booth* here?" His tone was so incredulous, and so hopeful. I share with that stranger the hope that someday the Christian and gay communities will share many members.

— J.Y., COLUMBUS, OHIO

"I AM TORN"

I was literally raised in the church. My father is an ordained minister, my mother has served as a women's pastor, a children's leader, church secretary, assistant to the pastor, and more, and I was brought up with the idea that a huge part of my faith was service in the church. From the moment I was allowed, I was serving in children's church, the office, youth programs, ushering, prayer teams, and more. I went on Missions trips; I led people to Christ; and I helped people grieve as they went through the worst life has for us. At times I wore the title of pastor, but for the most part I just lived it.

Yet, all through those times, I kept a huge secret to myself. I am queer. I am attracted to men and women; I am bisexual.

I haven't told my parents or any other family members because of how tightly they hold to the most conservative teachings. I don't want to lose them, and because I am bisexual can pass for straight when I have to. It's still a huge toll on my life. Hiding a part of myself, just to keep my family in my life.

As a child, I distinctly remember hearing several sermons from the head pastor about how "it isn't joyful to be gay." There weren't any gay people that I knew of in our church. I was the only one I knew who was fighting those urges. Did he know? Was he preaching from the pulpit just to convince me to turn from my sin? He had to be. If he wasn't, then why else would he preach that message? That same message was reinforced at youth camps, where we were taught what natural expressions of love and physical intimacy were—and told that if we had any unnatural urges, we should come forward to be prayed for, to be cleansed by Christ. Most of us boys came forward, ostensibly because of our masturbatory habits—but in my heart, I was asking to be freed from those desires that my pastors kept telling me were sinful. I kept asking, kept praying, kept crying out to my God—but the only answer I got was silence. My God, who answered other prayers, who acted in my life in ways I could not doubt, simply did not answer my prayers to take away those urges.

Did He want me to resist them on my own? Why wouldn't He help me?

Year after year of fighting my own urges led to quite a bit of depression, until at university, I met a Methodist reverend. She was a firebrand liberal, outspoken in her calling for equality, justice, love, and peace. She showed me scripture after scripture, new translations, and supporting documents and scholarly work that refuted everything my pastors had always taught me. Of course, I insisted on doing the research myself. I even taught myself basic biblical Hebrew and Greek, and sought out rabbis and priests. In the end, I learned she was right. Being queer was no more a sin than being straight.

When I finally decided to come out to some people, mainly friends in college and coworkers, most were supportive. But I remember one very conservative friend who pulled me aside.

"You really are going to hell, you know," she said in the blandest tone possible. "Even if the gays and lesbians can't stop themselves, you are choosing to sin. You choose to sin with other men, when you could choose to have a normal, loving relationship with a woman."

I tried to reason with her that an orientation such as mine isn't a choice, that I don't walk around choosing who will catch my eye anymore than she did. But it wasn't worth the air it took to speak.

In my life, I am out to my friends, my coworkers, and most people I meet. But I keep back that portion of myself from my family because

I fear that they will have the same reaction my former friend did. I'm afraid they will judge me for something they can't understand.

On the reverse side, living in the queer community as an openly religious man, I draw just as much flack from my queer friends. They say I'm trying to hold on to the past, that I want to desperately keep that bit of normalcy, that I am betraying the community by keeping my ties with my faith.

As a bisexual, liberal Christian, raised by Southern Baptists and living in the Queer Ghetto of an urban center, I am torn.

— J.H., SEATTLE, WASHINGTON

"I WAS THE WORST OF THE WORST"

I grew up in the church. I have many positive memories associated with the churches my family attended, and I took ownership of my faith at an early age. But there was also an unacknowledged aura of fear in those conservative congregations: fear of hell, fear of the world, fear of the fiery wrath God might at any moment unleash upon our sinful nation.

That fear had to be vented somewhere, and there were plenty of targets to be railed against: Hollywood, liberals, Catholics, rock music, abortionists, secular humanists, and, last but certainly not least, homosexuals. Gays were the worst of the worst, sinners of the most perverse sort who hated God and actively sought to destroy civilization.

Given that understanding, I had no context in which to understand the feelings I began developing when I hit puberty. I loved God, loved my country, and sought to live a clean life. So I certainly couldn't be one of those terrible monsters that all the preachers so angrily condemned.

Instead, I simply didn't acknowledge the interest I had in other boys. I really didn't understand why my friends would turn into such idiots when around girls that they liked, but I figured I was just better than them at resisting temptation. Adam went with Eve and not Steve, after all, and I even had a "crush" on a female classmate in eighth grade (though truth be told I never once thought of kissing her, much less doing anything even more physical).

I never went on a date until I was in college, and even then it was never more than asking a female friend to accompany me to a couples-oriented event. By the time I was twenty I began consciously realizing that something was very wrong with me, but I was able to rationalize it as a developmental issue; a little more male bonding, I told myself, and I'd eventually grow out of it. The Christian college I attended was enlightened enough to acknowledge that homosexuality wasn't a choice, but it was considered to be a purely psychological condition.

By the time I was in my mid-twenties, it was becoming harder to keep all of my feelings buried. Finally, during a period when nearly all of my college friends had moved away, and I was as isolated as I'd ever been in my life, I was forced to consciously acknowledge the fact that I was attracted to men, and that those feelings weren't going away.

I was still too afraid to talk to anybody I knew, so I tried to find help online. In the mid '90s, the web was just barely growing beyond the novelty stage, however, and online resources were still few and far between. Gay-supportive theology was still in its early stages as well, and what little I did find sounded to my staunchly conservative ear like weak attempts to rationalize a sinful lifestyle.

That summer I began attending a new church, and on my second week there, the program contained an advertisement for a Living Waters program that a member was about to start. It took me two weeks to work up the nerve to call the number listed in the program. To this day, I don't doubt that God led me to that group, if only because a program like that was the only way I was ever going to open up to another human being about what I was going through. And the healing I experienced as I began talking for the first time about this huge piece of me was life-changing. In addition to the other guys in my group, I shared my "struggle" with my mother and several close friends.

At the same time, however, Living Waters instilled me with a lot of false hope for changing my orientation. I still very much hated that part of myself, and clung to the program's promise that I could begin growing into my "natural heterosexuality" over time. And in the initial flush of enthusiasm from the healing I was experiencing, I believed that I was already changing. I still didn't have the slightest interest in being physically intimate with a woman, but I was so convinced it was only a matter of time that over the next several years I made several attempts to date.

I also developed a strong circle of friends outside of the program (friendships with heterosexual men were encouraged), and for a brief period of time drew a lot of strength from those relationships. As each of them met their future wives within a relatively short period of time and drifted away, however, I quickly found myself on my own again, vaguely disillusioned that God had brought these great friends into my life, only to take them all away again.

Even worse, I'd fallen deeply in love with one of those friends. At the time I didn't realize exactly what I was feeling (and wouldn't have acknowledged it if I had), but letting go of him after he got engaged was one of the most painful experiences of my life. Falling back on the coping mechanism I knew best I withdrew again (which only made matters worse, when the next community group I joined at church turned out to be rather dysfunctional.)

Two years later, I was more than ready to move when an employment opportunity arose back in my home state. Those first few years after the move were lonely ones, but it was still a relief to leave behind what had become an unhealthy situation. I was still attracted to men and not women, however, so I decided to give therapy another try, this time through a program aimed at sexual addictions. It wasn't a perfect fit, but since ex-gay theory regards homosexuality as something akin to a sexual addiction, I was considered to be just another broken struggler by the program (SALT, created by the same ministry that started Living Waters).

When that program failed to produce any changes in my orientation I began searching for another. I ended up at a local ministry with a different approach to "sexual brokenness": this one had no fixed curriculum, but focused on building community (with everyone, not just straight men) and on relational issues. In that environment, which emphasized personal honesty over shoehorning one's story to fit abstract ideas about "truth," I began to unpack all of the anger I'd harbored toward God (both for the way I turned out and for the friends he'd given me just to rip them away from me again), and toward myself.

Unpacking all of that anger and grief was an intense and painful process (and more than a few times during it, I expected God to strike me down at any moment), but once I got to the end of it all I was able to hear from God more clearly than I ever had in my life. For the first time I was really able to hear God tell me that he loved me exactly the way I was; he didn't merely tolerate me because of the rules he'd set up, and I didn't have to become someone else in order to earn his acceptance.

As that revelation began to sink in, I was able to begin accepting myself for the first time in my life. It wasn't long, though, before new questions began bubbling up. If God can delight in me while I'm still fully homosexual, then why all the condemnation that the church had drilled into me for so many years? If I can experience emotional and spiritual wholeness without first changing my orientation, what else have Christians gotten wrong in their assumptions and conclusions about gay people? If the church could be so wrong about this, what else might it be wrong about?

The questions that kept pouring out frightened me, but I couldn't ignore them any more than I could stop breathing. Fortunately, I found others at the ministry who were asking similar questions, so we were able to talk through them together. I asked God repeatedly to stop me before I went off the deep end and became a full-blown heretic. But if anything, God seemed to be encouraging my questioning, even when I directly challenged him and everything I'd ever been taught about him.

It was disillusioning at first to discover how quickly everything I'd been taught about homosexuality fell apart under scrutiny. But it was also a relief to realize that being gay didn't mean I was mentally ill and doomed to a shortened lifespan, or that I was any less capable than "normal" people of building healthy, enduring relationships. When studied more carefully, it became clear that Sodom's destruction had nothing at all to do with homosexuality, and that the other verses used to condemn gays addressed contexts specific to the cultures of the time. The Bible's surprising silence on the issue as we understand it today still left a lot of room for varying conclusions, but perhaps that was an answer in and of itself.

I'm not sure how to sum up the countless hours of reading, journaling, blogging, conversing and praying upon which I embarked except to say that, if anything, my faith in God is now stronger and more mature than before. In the process of questioning everything, I've watched the Bible come alive as I learned to read it on its own terms; it has become for me the story of God's relationship with his creation, rather than a divine rulebook.

Many of my questions only led to more questions, but, far from discouraging me, I began to understand that this life isn't about having all the answers. The opposite of faith is not doubt, but certainty. Learning to embrace doubt and the humility that comes with not having all the answers has served to deepen my faith in God, and to increase my confidence in those conclusions I have been able to reach.

That's not to say that my life has become perfect. As healing as it's been to have more people in my life to whom I'm out, there are still a number of family members and old friends who don't know that I'm gay. This is partly due to my work situation (until earlier this year I worked at an evangelical organization), but also because I really don't care to endlessly rehash arguments that I've already settled for myself, and that I know will, in many cases, only fall upon deaf ears. Perhaps that's an attitude I need to work on, but for now it's enough that I have the love and support of my immediate family and close friends.

I've also become involved in a fully inclusive church. It seems so obvious now that church should be a place where everyone can be loved and accepted as they are, but in most evangelical churches—even many that consider themselves welcoming to everyone—an attendee who happens to be gay is viewed as a second-class citizen at best. I know many gay Christians who continue to worship God in such an atmosphere, but it's stifling and suffocating in ways that most straight Christians can't imagine.

I don't know what my life will look like ten years from now, or even one. But I see God moving in ways that I wouldn't have dreamed possible just a few years ago, and I'm excited to be a part of that. The body of Christ needs its gay members, and that restoration process has already begun.

— E.G, DENVER, COLORADO

"LYING AND HIDING"

My doctor said it had been a while since we checked my cholesterol, so I agreed to the blood check. Something in me (today I believe it was the Holy Spirit) prompted me to say, "I don't think there's a need for worry, but let's also do an HIV test too." I had known four guys who died of AIDS, but in my denial I thought I'd been safe enough … "safe enough"… through all those years of sneaking in and out of adult bookstores and bathhouses. And yet every week I'd still show up faithfully to the ex-gay Bible study group or Homosexuals Anonymous meetings. Most times at those meetings I'd have to confess I had been weak, and "stumbled" again. But all along—in my habit of denial and playing with fire—I still thought I'd been "safe enough."

The doctor's office called me on Friday.

"Your test results are in," they said. "The doctor would like you to come in and discuss them." They had an opening Monday morning, so I had the weekend to wait.

Monday, November 25, 1996, I heard my doctor say the words, "Well your cholesterol is looking good. But I need to let you know that your HIV status has changed." I went numb. Even though I had no symptoms or illness, the only thing that went through my mind was that I was going to die. The new "super meds" had just made the news that year, but I was only vaguely aware of them. With my denial almost complete, I'd successfully avoided reading up on anything to do with HIV/AIDS. I didn't want to know. I didn't need to know. After all, I'd been "safe enough."

With a T-cell count of only 54, and a moderate viral load, I was prescribed a cocktail of meds right away. I got a glimpse at the lab report. Written in the diagnosis box at the bottom: AIDS. And yet my doctor couldn't say that to me; just, "Your HIV status has changed." (I later learned that anyone with a T-cell count under 200 was automatically classified as having full-blown AIDS according to CDC standards at that time).

I panicked, barely getting home before completely falling apart. The only prayer I could get out of my mouth was, "Please, God. Don't let me go through this alone."

I called my best friend, who went with me to the pharmacy. I didn't want anyone to know about my condition, and so was afraid of buying my drugs through my employer insurance: how could I be sure the news of my condition wouldn't somehow reach my co-workers? I wasn't thinking rationally. I just knew I had to get the meds. So I charged the cost of them to my credit card: $1,600 for a one-month supply.

Having filled my prescription, the pharmacist knew what was going on with me, of course. He looked at me with a sadness I hadn't seen in him before. Gary was his name. He knew me by name, too; he also knew that I worked at the very high profile *Christian* theatre company just across the street from the pharmacy. I'd performed in front of thousands of people on that stage (including him), and in churches across the country.

Panic struck me again. I thought if news of my HIV status came out, it would ruin the ministry of our theatre. I would embarrass and shame the company and its well-known founder. She and her husband had invited a few of us in the company to Thanksgiving dinner in just two days.

At that dinner I tried to make small talk, and act as if all was well. Meanwhile I was thinking only of how to sneak taking my pills without drawing attention to myself (they had to be taken with food at a particular time), and hoping that, as I had been doing the previous two days, I didn't have to throw-up.

Still in panic mode, I thought that I should tell the founder of our theatre about my condition, and at the same time resign. She agreed to meet me at her office the next day. There I spilled it all, along with a bucket of tears. She'd known I struggled against homosexuality, and had supported me in the "ex-gay" path. But now I had to admit to her that I wasn't successful in that struggle, and the cost I now had to pay for it.

Of course, I told her, I would resign from the company.

"Why do you have to resign?" she asked.

"I … well … because … uh … if this gets out, it would ruin this ministry—"

"How long has it been since you've been active in the lifestyle?" (Ugh; the *lifestyle* line.)

I lied, and said three months.

"If someone wants to be in this ministry, and is not active in that lifestyle, there's no reason for them to go anywhere. If you *are* active in that lifestyle, I'd have to let you go. But I believe in you. And God believes in you. And I don't believe you're going to die. It may even be that this is the time you've been born again."

I couldn't believe it. I was being loved, not thrown away.

That week became the watershed moment of my life

In the twelve years since then I've turned from lying and hiding, to standing under the cleansing shower of God's love and trying to commit to a life of honesty and authenticity as much as I know how to do. That pursuit of authenticity led to some important changes. I began the process of coming out to family and friends; I could no longer abide secrets, and so I chose to fully disclose to my immediate family. This was doubly painful to them, since they had to hear that I was not only gay, but HIV positive. I guess it may have cushioned the blow a little for them to hear that I was pursuing an "ex-gay" path—but that was about to change as well.

The pursuit of honesty begins by looking into the mirror of the soul. I had to first accept the fact that all the years of praying, crying, and pleading with God to change my sexuality had not, in that regard, made any difference at all. God had not "healed" me. I would never be "ex-gay," and so finally I chose to accept this reality as a fact, and to embrace who I really was: a gay man trusting Christ's finished work on the cross, a gay man striving to bring himself into full relationship with God.

I was also a gay man with AIDS who, day by day, was literally trusting God for his health. And for the first time in my life, I realized that God truly does love me *as I am*. I had always thought that the change I wanted was to be made straight. But the change God wanted me to experience was the healing of my heart from self-hatred and shame to joy and gratitude. I began to learn how to receive Christ's forgiveness, and how to forgive myself. The sense of freedom and peace this brought me was, and continues to be, unbelievable.

Full commitment to honesty and authenticity has not been easy. I often don't measure up. But for me there's no going back. I have been blessed beyond measure with friends who love me, a steady job with medical insurance, and, so far, reasonably good health. God answered that cry of my heart; I am not, after all, going through this alone. And yes, in a way, through all that, I was born again.

— L.W., Houston, Texas

"THE FALLOUT WAS HORRIFIC"

I'm a 23-year-old lesbian, and my parents are in no way capable of dealing with that fact. I was raised in a very conservative Southern Baptist household, and while my parents aren't crazy fundamentalists, they're just intolerant enough to think that being gay is the *ultimate* slap in the face to God. Years ago they learned that I was a lesbian, and the resulting fallout was horrific. I retreated out of cowardice, and in order to regain their trust lied to them that it was "just a phase."

The past three years have been horrible for me. I feel like I've stopped developing emotionally, because I'm trying to remain in this limbo of striving for their approval without fully committing to the kind of life they want me to lead: marriage, kids, church every Sunday, etc. It's all the more difficult for me because I truly love my parents, and can't conceive of giving up a relationship with them. They're kind, funny, smart people. I think being gay is the only thing I could possibly be that would absolutely devastate them.

I haven't given up being a Christian. But I've been really buckling under all of this, and I wish I had a person of faith around to talk to. But the pastors in this deep southern town aren't the progressive types. I just want to lay this burden down somewhere.

I don't know what to do at this point. I just met a girl I really like, and I'd like to move on with my life, and experience a healthy relationship with her. I can't do that in my current position, though. My father, whom I love so much, wants me to move back home and go to grad school at the university where he teaches. He thinks it would be good for me, and would cause him and me to grow closer. On some level, I agree with him about that. But another part of me wonders if it would be best for me to practice with my parents a scorched earth policy: if I should just tell them, once and for all, that I'm gay, and then stay away from them long enough for them to at least start getting over it.

I know what would happen if I moved home and told them about who I really am: they would be so, so hurt; and I would never be at peace from their efforts to save me. I would probably lie down and submit to them out of my feelings of guilt and love for them.

I can't believe this is what my life has turned into. How did modern Christianity get so fucked that a totally average girl like me, from an otherwise great family, has to feel this kind of pain, and cause my parents to feel it, too?

— J.B., LOUISIANA

"DEEP PAIN AND REJECTION"

The summer I turned six years old, my family often visited with friends some miles away. A teenage boy in that family and I would usually go through some fields and beside a creek most every evening during those visits. We would share together physical acts. I always looked forward to those times with him.

One Friday night when he wanted to leave our siblings watching television, I told him I wanted to finish watching the show. Later, he asked about my wanting to stay behind. I told him that at Vacation Bible School I had accepted Jesus as my savior. He never again asked me to the creek.

One therapist, when told of this when I was an adult, wondered how, back then, I had known that it was wrong for a child to have such encounters with an older youth. The answer was that, even at that young age, I knew that the spirit of God had spoken to my heart the truth that I had been taken advantage of, that such acts were to be only between two adults who were in a committed relationship with each other.

I truly wish I could say that through the years I had always been a mature enough follower of my Messiah Christ that I adhered to that insight. But loneliness, isolation, depression, rejection, and, truthfully, rebellion because of being so different, yielded times of giving myself away just for the security of a few moments of being accepted.

Life was always a terrible battle. I prayed literally thousands of times for God to change my desires. I also prayed just as often to be made willing to become willing to *be* willing to change, so as to be absolutely certain that I was doing all the correct things to be "healed" and forgiven of my "unnatural" desires.

I even prayed statements such as, *Lord, make me lust after a woman.* But it was all to no avail. That which the Church taught and believed continually battled against that which I felt and desired to understand in my heart and mind.

My heart, mind, and spirit questioned the Spirit of God: *If who I am, and how I feel, is so wrong and out of your will, why then do you bless my life by using my music, my writing, my teaching, and my speaking to encourage others, and to help them better understand their relationship with you. Why, God?*

I would plead with agony: *Why, Lord, would you call me, and anoint me to minister to others? If I were you, and I had an ambassador who was supposed to represent me, but whose life was totally misrepresenting me and my kingdom, I'd soon take him out of service—not bless him as a representative, as you have me.*

Years came and went, and I would continue to strive and struggle, as stated in this simple poem of mine:

> Yes, I am
> > No, I'm not. . . .
> Yes, I am
> > But I don't want to be. . . .
> Yes I am
> > And I'm glad.

Ultimately, I concluded that if "bitter water and fresh water" cannot come from the same stream (James 3:11), then I could not be too far out of God's will if God continued to use and bless me. I stood on the truth that God "formed me in the womb." (Jeremiah 1:5) God ordained my entire being —my essence of body, mind, soul, spirit; my temperament and personality—when God Created me at conception.

I concluded, "If God is for [me], who can be against [me]?" (Romans 8:31) I must answer to God for the life I lead. I cannot go by what modern-day Scribes and Pharisees believe and teach. (Ones such as they must answer to God for their life's actions and teachings of bitterness and strife toward gay persons.)

At times, I still think it would be a lot easier if I was not gay. But I also realize that if I weren't gay, I would be a totally different person than I am, and would not be able to touch others in the same way God now uses me to.

Throughout all these years there has been one thing, one hope, which has kept me from turning from the Church and ultimately from God: my own, personal *experience* with God through the spirit of my Messiah Christ. God has helped me deal with all the pain and conflict that most every gay person faces.

Experiencing the agape love of God—knowing that God accepted me just as I am; just as he created me—proved to be a foundation unshakable against the false teachings and attitudes I faced. I learned many years ago to stand firm, and to apply to my own life the words of Peter the Apostle: *"Lord, To whom would I go; You have the words of eternal life."* (John 6:68)

I lead a quiet life; one that is open and (if asked) honest. I strive to be Christ-like in every area of my life. I do not stand on a soap box and proclaim, "Repent, and be saved!" nor do I stand on a soap box and proclaim, "God loves gays, why don't you?"

When someone who knows me finds out I am gay, I usually tell them, "I'm still the same exact person as before; now you just know something about me that you did not know before." I try to give them time to adjust to knowing this information (not expecting them to immediately set off fireworks in glad hallelujahs of support), and trust that they will continue to treat me the same as they did before. I am happy and at peace to share with whomever desires to listen attentively—not argue or try to change each other—but to share, so that mutual support and a greater understanding can exist between us.

My hope is that those of us who are gay will accept that God accepts and desires a personal relationship with each of us; that God desires a unity of hearts between all believers, gay and straight, so that non-believers will intensely see God's love is available to everyone; that the word "hypocrite" will be removed from our language; that true unity will prevail.

I am grateful to God that I am created as I am. I continue to pray for greater trust and reliance on the Holy Spirit in order to live abundantly, as I have been made. God has given me—and all Christians who also happen to be gay—an opportunity to make a mark for the glory of Christ in the Church Universal and in society as a whole. The task is before me—before you. May we "press on toward the goal to win the prize for which God has called [us] heavenward in Christ Jesus." (Philippians 3:14)

It can be difficult to keep ridicule and the accusation that one is not a Christian if one is gay from causing deep pain and rejection. It can be difficult to keep these actions and attitudes from causing us to give up. Yet, as we each rely on our own personal experience with God through the Holy Spirit of Jesus Christ, we will be granted the "peace which passes all understanding." (Philippians 4:7) We will be imbued with the strength to endure to the end.

— D.S., KENTUCKY

"YEARS OF FEELING LOST"

Coming to terms with my homosexuality was like a shotgun blast to the face of my faith: it blew a dozen holes in it.

My journey began when I was twelve, with feelings I knew I wasn't supposed to have, at least not for the people for whom I was feeling them. And if there's one thing an evangelical learns, it's that you need to feel the right feelings. I suppressed those emotions for eight years, even as pastors and speakers begged those "who struggle with same-sex attraction" to come forward for prayer and eventual deliverance.

My spiritual mentor finally forced me to confront my feelings on a mission trip to Los Angeles when I was twenty. I spent the next few months trying to find a counselor whom I could afford, who was in my health insurance network, who could help me. After I experienced a taste of depression, though, I went to my on-campus counseling center, and was there paired with a counselor who (predictably) tried to help me come to terms with my feelings, rather than overcome them. I fought her. My goal was to *change* my feelings, not overcome them. What I wanted to feel were the *right* feelings.

That summer my parents confronted me about the lesbian-themed websites they discovered I'd been viewing (no, not *those* kinds of websites). I assured them over chocolate milkshakes (to ease the blow) that, yes, I had been experiencing feelings of attraction to other women, but that I was working on it.

That September they sent me to a Focus on the Family "Love Won Out" conference. And it was at that conference that I realized (I'm not sure why, probably because the whole thing was kind of creepy) that I didn't like these ministries that claimed they could change my feelings. I didn't, after all, *want* to change my feelings. I shouldn't *have* to change my feelings. From that point on I was able to start the difficult work of coming to terms with my identity as a gay woman.

It took another four years, though, before God healed the holes in my faith. More importantly, it was only after meeting my partner and experiencing romantic and physical love that I was able to fully understand what love is, and therefore what God is. Without her I would have come to terms with my sexuality and faith eventually—but it would have taken years longer.

I am a Christian, again, after four years of feeling lost. My homecoming was sweet. For the first time in my life, I know what it means to be a new creation. For the first time in my life, I know what Paul means when he writes, "The Spirit Himself testifies with our spirit that we are children of God." I know that the Spirit testifies with me, and it goes deeper, now, than mere emotions that I have.

Because I have the assurance of that Spirit (and the love and support of my church family), I can say to those who doubt that anyone who is gay can also be Christian that their problem is not with me, but with God. If they don't like the way I live my life, they need to take it up with Him.

So I say to my evangelical brothers and sisters, and to my family: look at the fruit! Jesus told us that we would know false prophets by the fruit they bear, that "A good tree cannot produce bad fruit, nor can a bad tree produce good fruit." My relationship has produced good fruit. Accepting my sexual identity has produced good fruit. Hiding and denying my sexuality produced bad fruit. As I've come into my identity as a gay Christian, I have donated more of my time and money than ever before to helping the poor. I have devoted myself more than ever to realizing the Kingdom of God. These are good, healthy fruits. They do not come from a diseased, deluded, or otherwise disordered tree. I am not diseased, deluded, or disordered. I am gay. And I am a follower of Christ. If you also are a follower of Christ, then you are my brother or sister; I love and welcome you as such, no matter what you may think of me.

— J.M., KANSAS

"DESPERATE TO NOT BE GAY"

I used to be an evangelical Christian. I received my seminary degree from Jerry Falwell's Liberty University, and was a youth pastor at a non-denominational mega-church. I also spent seven years in ex-gay ministries trying desperately to not be gay. You should see some of the things I wrote during that time. I thought that there was no possible way I could be gay and a Christian.

Yet, slowly, my theology started to change. I didn't change my theology because I was gay; I became okay with being gay because my theology changed. As an evangelical I had trouble seeing how others could possibly hold to their various theologies, when mine seemed so clearly correct. I wish that today I could tell every evangelical Christian that there are other theologies out there just as viable as theirs. Because I take a different approach to scripture or other topics than they do, doesn't mean that Christ is any less my savior and Lord than he is theirs. God is big enough to handle all of our differences. I hope that one day all we Christians are, too. Because there are so much more important things we should be focusing on.

— B.W., California

"I DESTROYED MY PARENTS' DREAMS"

I've always been a Christian, and my dad is a pastor, so I grew up in the church. Of everything I thought I'd be, I never thought one of those things would be gay. I first noticed that I was interested in boys when I started puberty, which was around seventh grade. In eighth grade I discovered the Internet, and started looking at porn. I did see some straight porn—where, again, I focused on the guy. So I decided to look for just dudes—and I liked it. I liked it a lot.

This continued for several months, until I slipped up once, and was discovered. I lied and cried my way out of it, and my parents eventually forgot about it. It wasn't until most of the way through ninth grade when I finally came out to myself—even though I knew I liked boys, it hadn't before really completely registered with me. And besides that, I had always been told it was wrong.

In tenth grade I came out to my friends and school—and no one really minded, although a good portion were surprised. So things went well for a while, and I came out to my mom on January 9th, 2010 at 9:07 a.m. I came out to my dad the next day. Things did *not* go well there. There were many nights of staying up late talking and talking about it, and then several months of "counseling" for me from an ex-gay "ministry." My parents told me that if I truly was gay, then I had destroyed all their dreams for my future—and that once I left the house I would be on my own.

Shortly put, my relationship with my parents got so severely damaged that now I am back in the closet. I hate lying to them, but any other course of action would cause too much pain on both sides.

Around this time I prayed to God to show me a sign indicating whether or not I was meant to be gay. Almost immediately I had this incredible peace and calmness come over me. It's hard to explain, but it was a feeling of *right*ness and confirmation. That feeling remains with me to this day. So now it's my goal to lay low until I go to college. At that point my parents will have little influence over me, and I can tell them the truth once and for all. Will they accept it? Probably not at first, and maybe never—but I'm not going to live a lie. What I do know is that I will never stop reaching out to them.

— M.C., North Carolina

"MY LIFE FELL APART"

I was the only child of a Nazarene pastor and his wife, who served as the church pianist. I never doubted their love for me. I loved my family, I loved my church, and I loved my God, whom I believed also loved me.

From the age of ten I knew I was different from other boys that I knew. They were starting to get interested in girls. All I thought about was boys. I was at church camp the summer I was twelve. One night, the camp chaplain talked about the sin of homosexuality. It hit home like someone had hit me in the head with a brick: I was a homosexual, and I was going to hell.

I spent the next forty years of my life in a constant battle between my being gay and what the church was teaching me. It caused me more pain than could ever be told. I knew at the age of fourteen that God was calling me into the ministry, to follow in my father's footsteps. I prayed each and every day to be "healed" from this terrible thing, to have God cleanse me from this sin of homosexuality. It never happened.

I was a licensed minister within the Church of the Nazarene. I was well known and well liked, respected by many across our district and denomination for my work with music and the youth of our church. Little did they know the constant battle that I was fighting. At the age of twenty-five I tried one final time to prove to the world, and to myself, that I was straight. I got married. I gave her the opportunity to back out before the marriage took place, by telling her about my homosexual feelings. She said that she wanted to help me become straight.

We were married, and we continued working in the church while I continued working towards my ordination. As the time for my ordination grew near, I confessed my homosexual feelings to an older pastor-mentor, and asked for his prayers as I prepared for a life time of ministry in the church. Instead of helping me and praying for me, he turned on me. He told me that unless I withdrew from the process of ordination he would out me and have me thrown out of the church. I could not imagine not being able to be a part of the church that I had grown to love. So with much sadness I withdrew from the ministry in the Church of the Nazarene.

I continued to work in the church over the next twenty years in many different levels, but mostly in the area of music. Despite what had happened, I still loved my church and my God, and would not turn my back and walk away. During this time my wife and I were blessed with three beautiful daughters, who, from the moment I laid eyes on them, became the most precious things in the world to me. I was still actively trying to get "cured" of being gay. Every day in my prayers I would ask God to heal me and take this sin from me. I even went to seek professional help, and had many sessions with a Christian psychologist. Nothing worked. I was unhappy with not being able to become straight. I was unhappy with my career choice, because I knew that I was called to be a minister. As a result I never stayed in one job for a long period of time. I could not be content not doing what God had called me to do. But what was I to do? The church taught that I, being gay, was a sinner, and as such was not acceptable to God and the church as a minister.

My life fell apart, piece by piece. My work fell apart. My love of the church declined to the point that it became a chore to go to church. My marriage suffered to the point of divorce, after twenty-four years of marriage. (Divorce is another thing in the Church of the Nazarene that is highly frowned upon.) At the lowest point in my life—no family, no job, no church, and nothing to look forward to—I turned to the only place I knew to turn: the Word of God. I began to read and study and search the scriptures like I never had before, looking for answers to what had happened in my life. For the first time in my life I was reading and asking for God to explain the scriptures to me, instead of someone else's ideas, or reading a commentary. It was just me, God, and His Holy Word.

Slowly, through prayer and study, I began to discover that I was *not* a sinner just because I was gay. God did not hate me because of who I was. As time went by, and the realization that God loved me just as I was began to take hold in my life, the years of doubt and self hatred began to fall away. Finally, at the age of fifty-two, after forty years of daily struggle, I became free. The day I stood up in church (not Nazarene) and said that I was gay, and knew beyond a shadow of a doubt that God loved just the way I am, was the beginning of life for me. A life finally free of the self-hatred and doubt instilled in me by the church. A life free to live the way God wanted me to, being the perfect creation that God created me to be.

I have lost my family through all of this. My family was always very conservative and church-oriented. All of my friends were in the church. When I came out, they all turned their backs on me. My own children have not spoken to me in over five years. It has been hard, but God has sustained me and helped me through it all. I knew of the importance of finding a church where I could fit in. I knew of the importance of church fellowship, and I still had the desire to be of help in the ministry of a church. After all, once God places a call on your life, you will never be happy until you say yes to Him, and fulfill that calling.

After lots of study and research online and visiting many different churches, I came upon the Metropolitan Community Church. I will never forget my first Sunday morning attending service there. I cried through the whole service. Every song was sung for me. Every scripture read was read for me. The sermon was just for me. The warm welcome I received overwhelmed me. For the first time in my entire religious life I cried in church—not, this time, because I felt guilty, but because I finally felt free, finally felt the true love of God in my life.

Since that service I have become a strong member of the local Metropolitan Community Church. I am involved in many different aspects of the ministry of the church. I go to each service, and feel the presence of God there, feel Him talking to me. Not condemning me. Not telling me that I am a sinner. But loving me, accepting me, and telling me that I am His beloved child.

— R.W., Palm Springs, California

"I HIT BOTTOM"

I'm a gay man. I have known I was gay for pretty much all of my life; I'd say that at around five I knew that I liked and had crushes on boys. I played sports, and did boy things like fishing, building forts, playing football with friends, etc. I also went to church with my family every Sunday and Wednesday, and to every revival that hit our town.

At an early age I gave my heart to Jesus, and asked Him to be my Savior. I confessed my sins and gave my life to Him. I sinned a lot as a child (or at least in my mind I did). I was raised in and around the hellfire Gospel, and was too scared *not* to be a Christian, to die and go to hell as a sinner. I prayed every night for God to forgive my sins, just in case I died that night, or Jesus came to rapture the Church.

As I grew, I became more and more aware of my gay feelings. I prayed for God to take them away, and to make me normal. I had preachers pray for me. I had "demons" cast out of me. I went to counselors. And still nothing: I was gay. That's when the (as I like to call it) bipolar Christianity came into play. I'd give up being gay for a while, and put all of my energy into being a Christian.

But the gay would always come back.

My Grandma Maxine always said that I was meant to be a preacher, and always encouraged me to become one. When I was twelve I attended a revival at the Methodist Church in Thomas, West Virginia. The revival's preacher, Reverend Michaels, came up to me after the sermon, put his hand on my shoulder, turned me around, and said, "Young man, the Lord has called you to be a minister. And you are going to answer His call?" And that was the official call of God on my life.

One small issue I had, though, was that I was still dealing with the gay thing, every day. I nonetheless went forward with my plans to become a minister, to give my all to God. I graduated high school and enrolled at Central Christian College, with the plan of becoming a missionary to Tanzania.

Over the years, however, the focus of my ministry kept changing. Then I had a turning point: I went through some things that eventually made me give up God, and to instead at least try to fully embrace my homosexuality. No matter what, though, God continued to be there with me. So I ended up again experiencing the "bipolar Christianity": I went back and forth between God and my other life.

Over and over and over I tried to pray the gay away. I begged God to make me normal. And guess what? I remained gay. I had a hard time approaching Jesus and God, because I kept hearing what I thought were their voices judging and condemning me. So mostly it was easier to just avoid them altogether, and to go out and have fun, living for the pleasures of life. But I wasn't truly happy doing that. I suffered from depression. I turned to drinking to medicate myself. I also turned to other vices to make me feel better.

Then, one day, I hit bottom. Nothing seemed to work out for me, and the more I tried, the deeper I dug myself under. That's when I decided—when I knew—that I had no other place to turn but God. So I prayed. And at that moment I no longer heard a voice of judgment from God. I felt from Him only love.

So, this is where I'm at. I've decided to allow God to work through me, and am now working again on becoming a minister. My first step is to take each day, one at a time, and to let Him guide me. I've learned for myself that God's grace is not earned, but rather given freely through his son Jesus. I know of a lot of people out there who feel that God does not love them because of who they are, because of what they do, because of where they are. I have been there and done that. I'm writing this to let you know that God's love is boundless. No matter where you are, who you are, or what you do, God loves you. And to my LGBT friends, and to anyone else who thinks you can't be Christian and gay? You are simply mistaken about that. You can be both. I *am* both.

God's love is boundless. He is all-powerful, all-present, and all-knowing. So how can we limit Him, and who He is, and whom He loves?

— L.H., Ft. Lauderdale, Florida

"ON SUNDAYS I'M ALONE"

I'm a woman. I'm eighteen years old. I'm Christian. I'm queer.
There are days when I consider myself lucky. When I realized
that I was something other than straight, there was no despair. There
were no desperate prayers for conversion. I acknowledged who I was
as a fact and moved on.

I had spent the better part of the previous year studying the Bible,
searching to understand why people who were born gay were still
condemned by God. I was emotionally in a place where desiring
women as well as men was perfectly acceptable within myself. The
only real concern was telling others, but outside of church, that
concern faded away as I came out to people. I knew that I had surrounded myself with loving, affirming friends who didn't give a care
about whom I liked, and that was enough for me to be comfortable—indeed, casual—about discussing my orientation with them.

One can be fairly confident that, in the general area where I live,
more people will be accepting of a woman who likes women than
won't. They won't glare at me if they see me holding hands with a
girlfriend, and they won't pretend that my love is any less legitimate
than theirs, or that I don't deserve the love I'm receiving.

Inside of church, however, it's a different story.

I look around my large Bellevue church, and I see heterosexual couples raising three, four, five kids to be heterosexual, sometimes to fit into old-fashioned gender roles (the man is the breadwinner, the wife stays home, etc.). I see Men's Group events about treating your wife (always your *wife*) well. And the singles group? Well, no one's going to go there seeking a same-sex partnership.

I see heterosexuals everywhere. Outside of church, it's no big deal, because I can usually turn to a gay friend who is literally right there, and know that we see the same world at that moment; it's a world in which we don't always feel like we fit, but that's okay, because we have each other.

On Sundays, I'm alone.

This hit me especially one particular service, when I had volunteered to read Scripture aloud with my mother. I was sitting at the front of the church, beside the pastors, when all of a sudden I felt a horrible wave of loneliness wash over me. Looking around, I didn't see a single person with whom I could confidently identify. They were all straight. I was queer. Barely anyone knew I was queer, and I didn't know anyone in church who was openly gay. Even in a church as large as the one I attend, I'm sure it would have gotten around if there was even one such person.

What was even worse was that I was in front of an entire congregation, alone, with no one to turn to. I couldn't contact my girlfriend for comfort.

Being alone when you don't want to be is probably one of the most awful feelings in the world.

I hope that one day I can be out and proud before my fellow Christians at church. I know that there is nothing wrong with me. I *know* that there is nothing wrong with me.

But when I am alone, I can't take the burden of a church's sadness. I just can't.

— S.L., Seattle, Washington

"I'M AN ABOMINATION"

I grew up in a very conservative Southern Baptist household. Everyone in my family, including all my extended family, is a devout Protestant. Many characteristics I now have as an adult are due to my evangelical upbringing. Some of them I value, and others I have spent my adult years trying to change. It was not easy growing up in a household where you learned that something about you, something that you cannot change, is not only wrong, but an abomination before God.

The earliest memories I have of "liking" boys instead of girls are from when I was four years old. I had a crush on one of my dad's friends at church. It wasn't sexual by any means, of course, but it was a very different feeling for me than the ones I had towards the girls that were my friends. I wanted to be around my dad's friend. Not because he was funny, or fun, or any other reason besides that I thought he was handsome, and liked sitting next to him during the service. From then on I have many memories of male friends, or friends of one of my family members, that I "liked."

I accepted the Lord into my life when I was six. I am now twenty-five, and remember the moment that I prayed for Christ to come into my heart as clearly as if it were yesterday. I understood exactly what I was doing. Of course, as I grew older I understood even more how wrong were my feelings for other men, and by the time I was twelve I would spend my quiet time crying and begging God to change me—to make me right. I didn't want to be wrong. I wanted to be a good Christian and not disobey God by having the feelings that I did. I spent all my teen years battling this. Sometimes my desires would prevail, and sometimes I would be able to ignore them. By having this constant battle in my mind and in my heart every moment of every day, I became completely emotionally erratic by my late teens.

The spring of my junior year in high school I came out to my older sister. She reacted by sobbing and saying she didn't want me to tell her what I had. That night my mother came into my room because she could hear me crying, and I told her I was gay. Her initial response was caring and understanding, but by the morning her Baptist upbringing had won over, and she told me that she was sending me to therapy.

The following year I met my first real boyfriend. For obvious reasons I didn't tell my family or friends about him. A couple of months into the relationship I introduced him to my mother as a friend, but it was obvious he was more. One night my younger sister found a text in my phone from my boyfriend and showed it to my mother. My mother did not react well to that. That night I went to my mother's medicine cabinet, found a prescription bottle, and took all the pills that were in it. Luckily it was only strong enough to make me very ill for a couple of days.

Of course by this point I had been all but exiled from my church. Right after I came out to my sister, she shared with a church member what I had told her. The following Sunday my youth pastor asked me into his office. He told me that he had heard what was being said about me, and that I was no longer on the church's praise team, and could no longer work in the nursery.

At the end of my senior year I joined the Army National Guard. The army offered me what I was looking for: money and a way out. Over the next twenty months I went back and forth about how I felt about my homosexuality. At times I would feel terrible guilt over it left over from my upbringing; other times I would feel completely secure in who I was. In August of 2005 I left for training for a mission to Iraq. I arrived in Iraq in October of 2005. This was one of the most intense learning experiences of my life. It was a face-full of reality. Life in that country is very different than it is in America. There is no way to understand the poverty without seeing it firsthand.

For the majority of the time I was there, I worked in a military detainment center. Halfway through my six-month tour I went home on leave for two weeks. While I was home I used my younger sister's cell phone ... can you see where this is going? One night while on leave I lied to my mother about where I was going for the evening. To make a long story short, she didn't discover that I had lied about that night until I was back overseas. The first time we spoke on the phone after I'd returned to duty, she told me that she knew about my lie that night. Only this time her reaction was much different than I expected. She told me that she accepted and loved me for who I am, and that she wanted anyone I loved to feel accepted and loved in her home. That moment between her and me will light my soul for the rest of my life. Without knowledge of what my mother had said to me, that very same night my older sister sent me an email begging for my forgiveness for how she had reacted to me coming out to her, and telling me she accepts me and loves me.

I cannot describe the difference in me as a man after this night. I'll just say that after twelve months in Iraq, the two closest people to me in my life accepting me, and one *very* near-death experience, I finally and truly knew who I was in the world.

I returned home in November of 2006, and in spring 2007 moved to New York City to study musical theatre at the American Musical and Dramatic Academy. Two months after moving to NY I met the most classy, well spoken, intelligent, cultured man I have ever met in my life. I have been with him for four years now. We lived in NY for two years while I finished school, and then we moved to Mexico, his home country, where we have now lived for two years. I love my partner with all my heart and soul; I am bound to him for life. We would be living in the U.S., but that I love and am fully committed to him isn't enough to allow me to sponsor him for a green card. If he were a woman it would be enough—but, oh well.

When I returned from Iraq I had learned two basic truths: 1. It's okay that I'm gay; it is not a sin; and 2. I need God in my life every day. Since I returned from service, God has been a consistent part of my life. I won't lie and say that's true every single day. I wish it were, but sometimes I just get so caught up in my own life that I forget Him—until I need Him again for something. But that's not because I'm gay; it's because I'm human. I love my Lord and speak to Him often. I still read my Bible. I still pray for guidance and understanding. I have seen the ugly face of judgment, so that is one thing I never want to do or be for others. Through my experiences I have learned a lot about being a Christian, and I learn more every day. The only thing I wish were different about my past is that I had more guidance in my walk with Christ. I felt very alone and very afraid for much of my life. That is not the purpose of Christians, or of Christ's Church. We are here to tell others about His free gift of love, yes, and to try and be more like Him. But above all we are here to love others in the way that He does: unconditionally.

— R.C., MEXICO

"IT WOULD BE ALL OVER FOR ME"

If a newspaper headline read something like HISTORIC DECISION: PRESBYTERIAN CHURCH TO ORDAIN LEFTIES, people would look askance, and ask, "So what? Who cares? What's the big deal, anyway?" But when the same headline uses the word GAYS or LGBT instead of LEFTIES, it's a whole different ballgame.

People used to be afraid of left-handed people. They were thought to be weird and different, perhaps evil or "of Satan." I have an uncle who was born left-handed, but my grandparents made him "switch": they forced him to learn something completely unnatural for him, something opposed to the way he was born, something over which he had no authority. (Now he's ambidextrous!)

But lefties, as it turns out, aren't, after all, wicked Satan-worshiping freaks of nature. They're really great to have on a baseball team! They have two hands just like everybody else, but they happen to use them in a different way than the majority.

So too with LGBTQ persons. We're still human; we're just like everybody else. We just use our bodies in a different way than the majority. Some people think they can change us, force us to "switch" to something completely unnatural for us, something opposed to the way we were born, in order to better accommodate ourselves to the norm. If you're of that persuasion, please wise up. We're not

Satan-worshiping freaks of nature. We're not sex-crazed maniacal predators ready to jump the next person we see.

I work as a lay minister for children, youth, and families, in a congregation that's part of the PCUSA which just passed an amendment authorizing the ordination of LGBT persons to the ministry. In a session meeting recently (*session* is the governing body of each Presbyterian congregation), one of our long-time members read a statement in which he resigned from his session post, and told us he was leaving our congregation and the PCUSA over this amendment. There were tears of shock and dismay, respectful encouragement to "agree to disagree," and a prayerful circle of blessing and laying on of hands before he walked out the door.

Despite this man's insistence that he is "not prejudiced" against gays and lesbians, I felt like I had been socked in the gut. Despite his consistent affirmation of me and my gifts over the time I have worked in this church, and the many times he has told me personally how grateful he is for my ministry and presence here, if he were to know that I'm not hetero, he would deny me that same ministry which he has readily supported in his assumption that I'm just like him.

Sorry, but how bullshit is this? One bit of information about my personal life would serve to effectively convince some people in my church that, despite the fruits they have seen and celebrated from my ministry, I should never have been granted the rights to that ministry in the first place. They love me! They know I do a great job! They praise me all the time for the new life I'm helping build in their children's and youth programs, and for the way I'm drawing the congregation together (they've been so scattered!). But the fact of my sexuality would immediately and irrevocably mitigate all that.

Poof. Ding. It would all be over for me.

There is *so much fear*, and so little education at work in situations like this. So many Christians, especially of an older generation, have never been in relationship (by which I mean worked collegially with, etc.) with someone whom they knew was openly LGBT. And until you have that experience, you're likely to be afraid.

"What are they like? Are they attracted to me? Are they thinking about having sex with me right now? Should I hide the children?" I can acknowledge these questions, because they were mine prior to my first being in a working relationship with a lesbian woman (and prior to my own realizations about my bisexuality). What I first knew about this woman was her warmth, intelligence, talent as a musician and minister, and her deep care for the earth. I loved and respected her—and *then* I found out she was lesbian. And that forced me to *think,* instead of just react.

I thought, "Wow. I've never met a gay person before, but I really like this gal, and she is a great friend, and I see what good she brings to those around her. So maybe what I've been taught to believe about gay people isn't correct. Maybe I need to re-examine my beliefs in light of my experiences." This, I believe, is one of the greatest ways humans are made in the image of God: we have *reason!* We can use our brains! So often I think Christians are conditioned to be automatons: teachers and pastors feed us doctrine and dogma; we swallow it all based on their authority and scholarship; we discount our own abilities to figure things out for ourselves. My reality in relationship with this woman contradicted what I had been taught. The teaching was someone else's, but the reality was mine. So I chose to re-order my life and my beliefs around what I had experienced and knew to be true.

This is not to say that I completely or in any way discount the authority of scripture or the Christian tradition. On the contrary, I began to incorporate reason as the third source of authority in the hermeneutic of my own life as a Christian disciple (my own tradition is Episcopalian: three cheers for the three-legged stool!). Faith is not the same as blind belief and uncritical acceptance. Why not test our faith and our beliefs to see if they corroborate our experiences?

Oh, wait: because we're *afraid!* Why? Because we think we don't "know enough" to be our own litmus tests. Hogwash. Dust off the ol' cerebellum and use it, for God's sake (literally!). God gave us brains so we wouldn't need to rely solely on what other people tell us. Revelation comes to each who is willing to find, receive, and consider it.

Anyway, back to my church. What lies before me is a dilemma. Stay quiet, keep my "secret" so I can continue to collect my paycheck? Or be true to my identity, and authentic to my nature—and risk the loss of my livelihood? The national denomination for which I work has made a formal declaration that ought to free me to reveal my true self to the congregation I serve. However, the national denomination is an institution, and I work amongst people, individuals who come together as "one" to fulfill our Great Commission. There are many within that group who would cast me out, eliminate me from the "one," if they knew I was bi. Surely "someone like that"—someone like *me!*—is living in sin, is a danger to our children, is unfit to set us an example of Christianity. Surely.

And yet every day I work to faithfully represent them, our church, and the God we share. And because of me they're grateful, and feel uplifted, and ministered to, and understood, and listened to. *Surely* they would not turn on me if they found out the truth! Would they eat their kind words to me? Take back their affirmations of my ministry? Ask me to leave? Deprive me not only of income, but also of doing the work that is essential to my identity, which brings me so much personal fulfillment?

This is the very hypocrisy that turns so many non-Christians away from the church: that the church, which is supposed to represent the love of Jesus, would so coldly turn away one of its own, one of its best (I say that with all humility and give the glory to God), one of those who love it the most.

This *hurts.* I've given my whole life to the church. I've been in one sort of ministry or another since I was three years old. And yet people in my own church, if they knew I was bisexual, would suddenly fear me, fear what I might be teaching to or thinking about their children, fear what I might suddenly start doing, fear what I am. It hurts because I am told to just shut up about it all, so that I don't rock the boat, or cause anyone to question my validity as a called lay minister, or (God forbid!) make anyone think that being gay is actually okay for Christians.

It hurts because people fling proof-texts at me as the temple priests flung stones at Stephen. It hurts because I have to *choose* between making a living doing what I love, or having the personal integrity to assert the truth of who I am. It hurts because other people's fear becomes the cause of my own fear for my safety and livelihood.

But "perfect love casteth out fear." (1 John 4:18) I refuse to live in, or be ruled by, fear. So while I'm not yet ready to out myself to my congregation, neither will I pretend that I don't support both the new Amendment, and those whom it has freed to now openly pursue formal ministry in the PCUSA.

That is my compromise.

Until such compromises are no longer necessary, I will stay busy in my church, trying to do justice, loving kindness, and walking humbly with God.

And perhaps I'll see you in church this Sunday.

— R.P., INDIANA

"I BEGGED GOD"

As a teenager, I did not especially like the chore of mowing the lawn in the middle of South Florida summers. But while doing so I would often converse with God. Countless times on paths back and forth across the lawn, I begged God to take away the one thing that made me unacceptable to Him.

"Why do I have this sinful compulsion to look at men?" I asked Him. "Why don't I feel attracted to girls?"

Not much was said about homosexuality in my church or family. But in the late '80s and early '90s, as I was entering puberty, I certainly understood that being gay was a bad, bad thing. It was a surefire way to go to hell. To make things worse, you wouldn't even get to enjoy being a sinner for long because you'd get your punishment on Earth, too: AIDS, being ostracized by the church, and causing your family shame. The message was clear; only heterosexual thoughts and actions are okay with God.

Who doesn't want to be okay with God? I sure did. So to *become* okay with God (being saved wasn't enough), the obvious next step for me was to surrender my sinful desires to Him, and allow Him to heal me. A pattern of surrendering to God, then being attracted to a guy, then questioning, and finally (having surrendered again, but this time in a different way), self-loathing again became the usual pattern for me. It especially established itself after my first sexual experience with a guy. The fact that I had been "intimate" with a guy horrified me. After all, I had a commitment to purity before marriage. Not only had I completely ruined that, I had done "it" with a male! I knew that if I didn't change I was headed down a path of destruction, and would be out of control in no time. I had already read Dr. James Dobson's book, *Preparing for Adolescence*. In it, Dobson writes, "Homosexuality is an abnormal desire that reflects deep problems, but it doesn't happen very often and it's not likely to happen to you."

That was just lovely to know. Not only was I a rare exception, I had deep problems. I didn't know what my deep problems *were*, though. I tried to deal with it all the best I could—which amounted to more of the surrender-guilt cycle. I figured that I must at heart be deeply rebellious (which is as the sin of witchcraft), because, after all, I was taught that if you're truly repentant, you *will* change. And I honestly did want to change. I had a pure heart about it. I wasn't just giving God lip service.

As a teen I would sometimes very cautiously sneak peeks at books about homosexuality in the library or book store. I wanted to understand both myself and how to become truly okay with God. Being conscientious, and not wanting to lose my relationship with God, most of my peeks were at religiously oriented books. I had been very heavily indoctrinated with the notion that anything outside of Christian thought was most likely a deceptive liberal attempt to draw people away from God. So I ended up reading books that led me to believe that my "deep problem" was my relationship with my dad and a lack of peer acceptance from males. These books contained great stories of men who had changed from gay to straight—and had the wife and kids to prove it! I was hopeful such a change was possible for me.

When I was about twenty-one, I decided to tell my parents about my attractions. I expressed to them that I had had sexual contact with a guy that was not continuing, and that I was not going to be sexual with men again. I told them that I believed that my desires for men stemmed from my lack of connection with my dad. They didn't really say much in response. My dad told me that I shouldn't mention anything of what I'd told them to my siblings, because many people go through an experimentation phase, and they didn't need to know about mine.

It was just a phase; and keep quiet about it. That was about it.

As I continued through college my attractions to men continued, despite the fact that I felt the air was clear between my dad and me. Furthermore, when I really thought about it, I knew that my relationship with my dad was better than a lot of other guys' were with their fathers. I didn't have the sense then to realize that if a paternal relationship was responsible for homosexuality, then there would be *way* more gay guys around. By then I was beginning to realize that I wasn't, in fact, just going through a phase—but I didn't dare call myself gay. That would be agreeing with Satan, and giving him a foothold in my life. I was determined to have victory over the sin in my life. I believed that I was a straight man who was just sexually wounded and could admit to myself that I struggled with same sex attraction. I had a problem, but not an insurmountable problem.

At this time I began attending a college and career group at my church. There I made several good friends. One of them was a nice young lady. We had fun teasing each other, debating scriptures, and simply hanging out. I realized that I liked her a lot. When I say "liked," I mean respected, admired, found her company enjoyable. I thought that perhaps I should start dating her. Being fearful of breaking someone's heart (and my own), I had already decided that early on in our relationship I would tell any girl I dated about my attractions to men.

I told this to my new love interest on our very first date. I know. Surprisingly, she was understanding about it, and did not reject me. Our relationship progressed as I studiously ignored red flags in my emotions and thoughts. I didn't enjoy kissing her, but rationalized that it was because I just wasn't into kissing. Maybe I'd be more into other aspects of the physical relationship. I thought that the reason why kissing a man had been so much better for me was because of sin's deceptive power over me. So I continued the relationship with the girl—and eventually, with a heart to please God and be accepted by my family and church community, I proposed marriage to her.

It should have been a sign visible even to me that rather than ask her to be my wife, I asked her to be my "best friend forever." She accepted.

Life—with the eventual addition to it of our three children—continued. The relationship of my wife and me never really took off or became very fulfilling for either of us. I kept hoping that as my love grew for her in our marriage, my attraction to her would follow. For several years I managed to perform sexually—thanks to the hormones raging within me—and to repress my desires to be intimate with a man. Actually, I didn't do such a good job of repressing those desires. Since the Internet was newly available, I was able to look at porn and chat with guys from time to time—maybe once or twice a month. I justified it as an outlet that allowed me to release my feelings and still remain physically faithful to my wife. I still hoped that one day I would kick this same-sex attraction thing.

Later in the marriage I became friends with a dear Christian man who listened to me pour out my woes. One day, after repeated conversations about my attractions, he stunned me by asking, "What if you *always* have these feelings?" At first I didn't want to acknowledge such a possibility. Yet, when I looked at the fact that I had done everything I had known to do, and was still attracted to men, I had to face reality. Praying, reading, developing my relationship with my dad, being friends with other guys, abstaining from porn, trying to "train my brain" by looking at women in pornography, focusing on the good qualities of my wife, and countless other attempts at heterosexuality had simply not worked. What was I going to do? I was heavily involved in my church's worship team. I went on international mission trips. If I accepted the fact that I was gay, and came out, I knew that Christians at my church would find unacceptable my continuing to serve God in those ministries.

For the first time ever, I earnestly started searching for what God really had to say about someone like me.

After lots of reading, studying, questioning, and praying, I came to know that what God says about me is that I am, after all, loved and perfect in His sight. I was finally able to discard all of the junk that most of my fellow Christians have blindly believed about homosexuality, and to accept God's 100% love and acceptance for me, and all that I am.

After that I could no longer continue to live the lie I had been living. I admitted to my wife that I still had homosexual feelings, and that I was done trying to change them. Of course she was angry, heart-broken, confused, and angry some more. After months of talking, we decided that divorce was the best option for us and our children. We did consider staying together for the sake of our children, but ultimately concluded that staying together would send the message to our children that it's okay to be inauthentic and basically live a lie. They would never witness what a functional, loving relationship really looks like.

Along with losing my family, I also lost the ability to serve in my church as the musician and singer I had been. I willingly stepped down from my volunteer church position, because I knew that once the news about me got out, it would cause problems, and our pastor would be put in the uncomfortable position of having to ask me to quit. I still desire to lead worship and participate in mission work.

Coming out as gay has caused me to question many aspects of the evangelical brand of Christianity. I have become a bit disillusioned and somewhat cynical about church as an institution. I know the majority of churches do great things for their communities and congregants. I just don't feel like I fit in, yet. Many people at my church know that I'm gay. They treat me with love, as Christians should. However, I don't feel truly accepted. I feel that they are loving me because it is their Christian duty to do so. I feel like they are just trying to build a relationship with me so that one day they can have "the talk" with me. Maybe that's my own issue to deal with.

Not too long ago, I was mowing the grass again. As I was pushing the lawn mower up and down the lawn, I began expressing my fears of and discontentment with both Christians and my adjustments to being an out gay man. I believe that in that moment God spoke to me.

"You know, here we are mowing the grass again," He said, "and still you are worried about your sexual orientation. I love you *just the way you are. Let it go.*"

So, every day, I have to practice letting go of the desire to be accepted by my Christian culture. I have to let go of other people's notions of God's plan for my life. I have to let go of the idea that I will never again be welcomed to sing in church or serve on a mission. I have to have hope. I have found that being gay, for me, is about letting go of my way, and trusting God with His.

— ANONYMOUS

"I ATTEMPTED SUICIDE"

I grew up in a Christian home. That would have been a wonderful thing (it certainly shaped me in many positive ways), except that the version of Christianity I grew up with was very fundamentalist and legalistic: no women speaking in church; women wear head coverings; no movies; no dancing, and most definitely no gays. (There was even controversy about welcoming African-Americans into our church, because it was located in Baltimore City, where during this time, in the '70s, the neighborhood shifted from mainly upper class white people to more middle class and poor black people.)

I accepted Christ as my savior around age five, but always struggled immensely with guilt. I didn't fit in to my parents' ideal of a girl child. I was a tom-boy, very strong-willed and extroverted; I seemed unable to "toe the line." Every night I would beg God to forgive me and help me to be good. I lived in tremendous fear of the second coming, of being left behind, of dying and going to hell.

When I reached adolescence I suppressed sexual feelings of any kind, having been told that they were sinful unless I was married. I dated a nice, Southern Baptist/Charismatic Christian boy, until I couldn't cope any more with the fact that while he really loved me, I didn't at all feel the same way about him. I broke up with him when I realized that he intended to marry me (he was eighteen; I was sixteen); I wanted him to be free to find someone who would love him the way he deserved.

Although I didn't really realize the nature of my attraction to girls, I tried *really hard* to be attracted to boys. When I left home to go to college, I went with my grandparents for a year to the same type of church in which I had grown up. But more and more I realized that I was not connecting with that type of faith. I continued to pray, because I wanted to be close to God. But more and more I felt that God was unhappy with me, and that there was nothing I could do about that. So, finally, I left the church, and over time abandoned Christianity altogether.

Fast forward several years, to 1995. I was attending medical school, and was in a relationship with a woman, N., whom I truly loved and wanted to marry. I was also starting to seek out God and Christ again. I received several gentle prods in that direction. One was a man I met around the same time that I met my girlfriend, a straight Christian who had no issues at all with a person being gay *and* Christian. That intrigued me, very much—but I still wasn't ready to return to church.

The summer of 1995 my mother and I went to Malawi, where my brother was living with his family. They were attending a Baptist church there, and on our first weekend with them we went with them to their church. During the service the pastor talked about "back-slidden Christians." His final words were something to the effect of, "If you have drifted away from God, I am praying that you will not sleep tonight until your heart is right with God again."

My mother and I were sharing a room, and that night, while lying under my mosquito netting, I thought about what the pastor had said. And I started praying. I asked God to show me the truth about myself, and about Himself. I told God that I was seeking a genuine relationship with Him, but that I just couldn't reconcile what I had been taught about my sexual orientation with what I had been taught about God. Then I listened and waited. And very shortly, I felt almost a *literal* embrace, like God was wrapping his arms around me. And I heard (not literally—but it was a real voice) God say to me, "I love you. I have always loved you. I made you the way you are." So I said, "But what about N.? What do I do about her?" "Love her," God said. "Just love her. I gave her to you to love." Almost immediately I felt peace. I slept better that night than I had for a long time.

After that night, I started reading the Bible to see what it *really* said about homosexuality. Upon reading Genesis 19, I felt great outrage over having been so long deceived. It was *very* clear that the story was not about homosexuality at *all*, but rather about gang rape. (And what was the deal with Lot offering his daughters to the mob of rapists?!) Even on my own, without the benefit of great Biblical scholarship, I started to see how my monogamous relationship with another woman was not addressed in any of the passages typically used to condemn such relationships. And in reading the Bible I was also reminded again of the love, hope, and grace offered by God through Christ's sacrifice for my sins.

When I returned to school in the fall, I set about looking for a church. I ended up feeling a strong draw to a Lutheran church that turned out to be very welcoming. Ever since joining that church I have felt very blessed by the Christians that God has put into my life.

I did, though, go through a very dark time after coming out to my parents and experiencing a PTSD-like reaction to their response to my revelation: to all their talk of my going to hell and being lost forever, etc. In the fall of 1999 I had a pretty bad breakdown; my partner N. left me, and I ended up attempting suicide, which landed me in a locked psych ward for a month. Meanwhile, my church community held me up, and helped me to experience God's love more fully. And my parent's attitude toward me started to soften (realizing how close you are to losing your child is probably a good wake-up call).

About a year later I met a Christian lesbian, and over time, she and I fell in love. I decided to move to Montana, where she was. We got married (twice: first a civil union in Vermont, and then in our back yard in Montana; both ceremonies were officiated by

Lutheran pastors long before they were really "allowed" to do that). God has blessed us with great love that draws us ever closer and closer together.

In 2006, I suffered a near fatal car wreck. My parents came to Montana and, miraculously, stood back and allowed my wife to fulfill her role as my healthcare proxy; they did not, for instance, resist allowing her to remain at my side in the ICU. It was a great time of healing the strained relationship between my parents and me. Today, both of my parents have embraced my wife as part of our family. My wife and I were also blessed with a child (we were in the process of adopting at the time of the accident; thankfully, I recovered enough to continue with the adoption), and my parents have accepted both of us as the mothers of their grandchild. (Each of us is, in fact, the legal parent of our child—miraculous in Montana!)

My parents also seem to be accepting the truth that, even though I am living in the relationship I am, I am still a Christian who desires to live according to God's will. I firmly believe that God put me in this family for a reason, and that more miracles for us all are unfolding each and every day. God has been with me through a lot of trials, and continues to bless my life.

— R.C., MONTANA

"THEY PUBLICLY PRAYED FOR MY DEATH"

I spent sixteen years as a fundamental evangelical Christian, trying to get God to fix me. I studied theology and Biblical counseling for three years in the hopes of discovering what I was doing wrong that was keeping God from answering my prayers to make me straight. I struggled with the guilt of same-sex attraction every day, and had no way of turning it off.

I was so despondent over my situation that I felt suicidal. I knew what was in store for me if I came out, but I was really at the point where I was either going to be a gay woman or a dead woman. Thinking about my two beautiful children, I knew that they would prefer a gay mom. So I did what I had to do. I just had *no* idea how bad it would get before it started to get better.

I came out to my fundamental evangelical husband almost four years ago. Initially, he was loving and kind. However, the church knew something was wrong, and when he told them what it was, I never had another civil conversation with him again. He came home from a meeting with the pastors and announced that the church was starting Biblical discipline proceedings (construed from Matthew 18) against me, and that the elders of the church would be contacting me. The elders came to meet with me at my dad's house to confirm that I was a lesbian, although I had not been unfaithful to my husband, or had any lesbian relationships during our marriage. They called me an apostate: one who knows truth but then chooses to turn away from God and reject Him.

I told them that I loved God, and did not reject Him. They believe in predestination, so I argued that if I was chosen by God then being a lesbian wouldn't keep me from heaven—and that if God didn't choose me I was going to hell anyway, so I might as well be happy in this life. They told me that I was going to hell, and left. Before exiting, they asked my husband to be sure that our two children were in worship service on the Sunday a few weeks later when they were having the Lord's Supper. In that public worship service, they announced my "sin" to the congregation, and invited everyone to contact me to let me know how they felt about my sin. The congregation was told they were not allowed to speak to me about anything other than my sin.

I praise God that my children did not make it to that service, as my dad took them up to his cabin for the day (where my ex was not able to locate them). I received angry letters telling me that I was hell-bound, including one from a twelve-year-old friend of my daughter. I got a visit from one woman who came by my house to speak to me about how I was grieving Jesus. She became emotional and lashed out, punching me in the face and bloodying my nose. I also praise God for sparing my daughter that sight.

My ex's church helped him hire a "Christian" lawyer to help him hide our assets. I had to borrow $2,000 from my father to hire my own lawyer. This man took my case, then never met with me until the day before my hearing. I didn't even know that I was allowed to have witnesses. The judge of our case was appointed by the governor of Georgia, who happened to be a Sunday School teacher at the same mega-church my ex's lawyer attended—where Johnny Hunt, then President of the Southern Baptist Convention, was pastor. And it was an election year.

I didn't have a prayer in my rural Georgia county. I lost my home, rental properties, custody of my kids, my dog, and everything else

I had ever worked for. The judge ordered me to leave with only my eight-year-old car and my clothes, until such time as the ex and I worked out an agreement. For the next two years my ex continued to argue with me over everything, so that I would go broke just negotiating, and give up everything to him. Before, I had been a home-schooling mom: I was a foster mom, hospice volunteer, church librarian, and I helped my ex with his house-flipping business. Now I had no home, no money, no education, no church, and no place to live.

All of the shunning and mistreatment of this "Biblical discipline" was intended to show me the Christian fellowship I was going to be missing out on. However, I was highly resolved not to go back to a life of lies and misery. My church had to "disfellowship" me off of their roster. In another public worship service, they prayed for the death of my sin, including my physical death. Yes, they asked God to kill me if it meant that I would not bring reproach upon the name of Jesus Christ. It was the lowest point of my life. Even my own mom and her evangelical family cut me out of the family. They refused to speak to me, and my mom said to me that she "hated" what I had become (a lesbian), and that I was a "despicable human being." I went to live with my Grandma, the woman to whom I was closer than anyone else in the world. She had been sick; we soon found out she had leukemia, and was given six to eight weeks to live. She made it almost three months. When she died, I thought I was going to join her. My heart was almost totally broken.

A few months after my grandma died, during my first Christmas without her, my mom's family had their usual Christmas gathering, to which I was not invited. They did, however, invite my ex to bring our children. My mom even took my ex and our children on a cruise. It was their way of punishing me for "choosing" my "lifestyle." My ex enrolled our children in a Christian school, where I was not allowed to take any part in their education; if I attempted to, the children would be expelled from their school. When I went to their school activities I was shunned and usually left sitting alone, a wide circle of empty chairs around me, as if I had a contagious disease. It was humiliating to be in a room filled with people I had once loved and ministered to, who now wouldn't sit in the same row of seats with me.

Knowing that I was now walking in truth for the first time in my life allowed me to hold my head high. At times, it was a bitter pill to swallow, but in the end, it showed me how it feels to be judged, and I thank God for that lesson. God never gives you more than you can handle, and what doesn't kill you really does make you stronger. My God has supplied all my needs according to His riches in glory. I have struggled like never before to make a new life for myself. I recently earned my AAS in Marketing Management (with a 3.95 GPA, thank you very much), and am now at Southern Poly getting my BA in Professional Communications. I just finished an internship for my local ABC affiliate, working as a segment producer on a local TV-show about non-profits. My college, so far, has cost me nothing: I've won three scholarships. I get side work cleaning houses, working as a professional organizer, and freelance writing for Atlanta's premiere LGBT bi-weekly newspaper, *The Georgia Voice*. (I even had a cover story with country singer Chely Wright last year!) I am madly in love with my wife, Melissa. We found a pastor who was willing to marry us; although we are not now legally wed, we wanted to make that commitment to each other, and to God.

I love Jesus. I love His teachings. I am passionate about reconnecting LGBT people with God, and I hope to be able to earn a living at being an activist, speaker, and motivator in this line. Either way, God has restored to me everything that was lost, and more. How can I be bitter or complain when I now have the life that I always dreamed of?

— S.H., Atlanta, Georgia

"THE CHURCH HATED ME"

"Your old mentor told me you struggle with lesbian feelings," my new mentor said to me.

I shrugged. All I could think was: *Not any more.*

My "struggle" with lesbian feelings had ended shortly before I became a Christian. I had finally accepted the fact that I am gay. *(I'm sick of lying,* I wrote in my journal, *of having a gulf between what I think and what I say.)* I started to come out to people, and then I had an encounter with Jesus. I've always believed that there was a connection: once I was able to accept myself for who I am, I became able to accept that God loves me for who I am.

I have never believed that God has a problem with my being gay. In fact, for my first two years as a Christian I attended a conservative evangelical church. Evangelicals are very welcoming people. A friend had invited me along to the church months before, when I first admitted that I was looking into Christianity, and their warmth and enthusiasm at my presence kept me there. There was plenty I liked about that church: the structure of the worship service, the vibrancy of the young congregation, the in-depth Bible teaching.

And yet it was hard. It was so, so hard. You see, almost the entire time I was attending that church (twice a week for two years), I had a girlfriend. Because I was supposed to be "struggling with my lesbian feelings," I knew I couldn't tell anyone. No matter how nice my church friends were, I could never be truly close to them, because to do so would mean lying with my whole life.

Oh, there were other gay people there; but they all took the view that we had to remain single and celibate. They held that anyone who thought they could be in a homosexual relationship and still be a Christian was deluded, and should be ejected from the church for their own good. Being a happy, out, loved-up gay Christian? Not an option.

It wasn't only the gay thing that made it so hard. It was the attitude toward evolution (*I am so sick of people trying to create controversy over stuff that is incontrovertible. But don't listen to me, because my girlfriend and I are going to burn in the eternal hell-fires for being unrepentant practicing homos, which is the one thing Jesus cannot forgive*, I wrote in my journal). It was the gender essentialism that prescribes particular behaviors for all women (*I cannot accept the idea that God is a misogynist, especially the insidious kind that couches the misogyny in non-threatening rhetoric about Christ-like submission to male headship*). Week in and week out, the constant low-level homophobia and misogyny felt like it was corroding me.

It wasn't an ocean of hetero-normative patriarchal bullshit: it was a slow and steady drip. And it took its toll. I began to think that the church, as an institution, fundamentally hated me. I read and reread my copy of *Bullet-Proof Faith* by Candace Chellew-Hodge. I evaded my mentor's attempts to engage me in discussions about homosexuality.

And, finally, I left the church. I spent the summer traveling around Europe with my girlfriend, reading the Bible every day, and praying and meditating a lot. It was the best thing I could have done for my spiritual life. It reminded me of a crucial fact: God is not the church, and the church is not God.

I'm starting a master's degree in progressive theology. I'll be studying scripture (which my old church would approve of) through an assortment of post-modern lenses (which they would not). I don't regret my two difficult years among evangelicals, because I know I'm one of the lucky ones—I survived. I dearly love you, my evangelical brothers and sisters, but I want you to know: In your slavish adherence to the letter of the text, you are completely, utterly, and totally missing Jesus' point.

— A.T., LONDON

"ANGRY AND ASHAMED"

I'm a 32-year-old South African lesbian mother of two young children. I'm the youngest of four children; my parents had a fifty-percent success rate (my brother is also gay).

I grew up in a very conservative Christian home, where we were taught that being gay is a sin, and an abomination to God, and that all gay people go straight to hell—no passing "Go," no collecting two hundred bucks. So when I realized that I was a bit "different," I tried to force myself to think and feel as a normal girl. I did my best to think that it was all just a phase I was going through. I wanted that to be true.

I didn't have a very happy childhood. Dad was an alcoholic (up until five years ago). I was sexually molested at the age of about five or six. I'm also a rape survivor. So I believe that I have had my fair share of the crap of life.

I was married to my then-best friend. That marriage lasted for eight years.

My brother came out to my family about seven years ago. It didn't go down very well. My family didn't accept what he told them about himself: instead, we all had to pray for my brother, so that "the demon of homosexuality can leave his body."

I came out to my family only about one year ago, and World War IV broke out. My sister (who is married to a pastor) thought it was her duty to read all the clobber verses to me. I was even told to give my children up to my ex-husband, an adulterer who lives with his mistress and the child they had out of wedlock, because not doing so would mean destroying my kids' lives. I was told that I had exchanged "one heap of crap [my ex-husband] for another heap of crap [my girlfriend]," by people who had never met my girlfriend, nor spoken a single word to her.

I tried to stay positive throughout all this, and kind of drifted away from God. I was angry and ashamed of who I was. I joined a lot of Internet groups to help me feel better about myself and to answer all my questions. But I still felt as though I couldn't get anywhere. That's where you came in, Mr. Shore. I found your link on one of the sites I visited, and started to read your blog.

I'm now at a place in my life where I can freely pray to God about my life and my relationship with my partner without feeling guilty or ashamed, and where I can stand before Him knowing that this is who I am, and that He made me perfectly. I am free to love, be loved, and enjoy life for once. No one can change me, pray me out of this "lifestyle," or chase the "demon of homosexuality" out of me. This is me!

— M.P., SOUTH AFRICA

"I LIVED 30 YEARS ALONE"

I am a 72-year-old Christian mother and grandmother. I had a wonderful career as a teacher for every age, from pre-school through college. I served as a member of our church council, as a Sunday school teacher, as a Vacation Bible School superintendent, and I have been on mission trips to every continent. My hobbies are studying, reading, travel, genealogy, gardening, and dogs.

I am a lesbian. For most of my life, I hid that part of who I am, deeply in denial. I did not choose to be a lesbian, but I did choose to deny that part of myself, in the belief that I had to choose if I wanted to follow Christ. From the time I was seven years old, I wanted, most of all, to follow Jesus. As a young teen, I wanted to be a pastor, but I learned that "girls couldn't do that." I got married because that was what was expected of me, and I tried for fifteen years to make that marriage work.

Then—out of the blue!—I fell deeply in love with a woman with whom I worked in ministry at our church. The day came when we spoke to each other about our feelings. As we shared our hearts together, we learned that we both had felt something of these forbidden feelings since childhood, and had kept them hidden. But we felt so perfect together; and we began to believe that God had brought us to the place we were.

Oh! Then we were found out! We were threatened with losing our children (my four children, and her son). Our children were told that we were filled with evil spirits, that we were an abomination to God. We were counseled in ways that filled us with fear and shame. We were convinced that we had to choose God and our children, and give up our love for each other.

With broken hearts, we went our separate ways. We began to try to restore our children's trust, along with our relationship with God and with our church. We moved to different towns so that we couldn't see each other.

For the next thirty years I lived alone. I was never fully successful in restoring my children's love after what they went through, but I was able to develop a good career, and to serve in Christian ministries in my church. As a single Christian woman, I was free to do volunteer work, travel, and work on genealogy. Although my heart ached for the loss of my children's love, I was able to go on, trusting and loving God, and continuing to hope that "in all things God works for the good of those who love him, who have been called according to his purpose."

For all of my adult life I spent New Year's Day in prayer, seeking God's direction for the coming year. Each year I ended the day with a strong impression of someone for whom to pray, and some special need for ministry. I would write it in my Bible, and at the end of the year, I could see how God had worked.

But on New Year's Day four years ago, after a long day of fasting and prayer, I sensed God's message: "This time it's not about someone else. It's about you. You need to be honest with yourself about who you really are."

And I knew it was time to do something I had ignored and denied for thirty years. I walked over to my computer and Googled "Gay Christian," not knowing what, if anything, would appear.

And suddenly the pages opened up. I read for hours, learning about better Bible translations, learning about organizations for welcoming gay and lesbian Christians. With tears of joy and relief I learned that I didn't have to hide that part of who I am anymore. I could admit to God, and to myself, without condemnation, that I am a lesbian. A huge burden was lifted from me.

I had no intention of changing anything of my outward life or relationships. I was single and content. But I decided to tell my children, and they made the decision to remove me from their lives and from the lives of my grandchildren. They continue to believe that being gay or lesbian is a terrible sin, and that they must protect their children from me.

Now, little by little, I am beginning to realize that I need to "come out" as a lesbian Christian. While I have lost my family, I have found a church that is welcoming. I am still not out to most of my neighbors and friends. But I am beginning to understand that coming out as a Christian lesbian may be a new way to love and serve others. And I continue to hope and pray that someday my family will be restored to me.

— R.W., SEATTLE, WASHINGTON

Essays by John Shore

What Would Jesus Do If Invited to a Gay Wedding?

I've recently been invited to a couple of gay weddings. So—what with being Christian and all—I asked myself the famous question, "What would Jesus do?" (Which I don't too often ask myself, actually, since Jesus could, for instance, raise people from the dead and turn water into wine, whereas I can barely drag myself out of bed in the morning and/or turn water into coffee. Safe to say many of His options are none of mine.)

Wondering what Jesus would do if he were invited to a gay wedding naturally led me to the New Testament. And therein I found these quotes from Jesus himself:

> Woe to you, teachers of the law and Pharisees, you hypocrites! You give a tenth of your spices — mint, dill and cumin. But you have neglected the more important matters of the law — justice, mercy and faithfulness. You should have practiced the latter, without neglecting the former. You blind guides! You strain out a gnat but swallow a camel. (Matthew 23:23-24)

and

> Woe to you, teachers of the law and Pharisees, you hypocrites! You shut the kingdom of heaven in men's faces. You yourselves do not enter, nor will you let those enter who are trying to. (Matthew 23:13)

and

> Woe to you, teachers of the law and Pharisees, you hypocrites! You travel over land and sea to win a single convert, and when he becomes one, you make him twice as much a son of hell as you are. (Matthew 23:15)

and

> Love your neighbor as yourself. (Mark 12:31)

When I next went looking for anywhere in the Bible where Jesus says anything—and I mean *anything*—about homosexuality, I learned that Jesus spent about as much time talking about gay people as I do talking about the belly-buttons of seahorses. Of course, it's entirely possible that Jesus *did* say many crucially informative things about gay people, but that when he did so no one around him happened to have handy an ostrich feather, sappy stick, or whatever it was they used for pens back then. Which would make sense, actually. If you've spent any time at all reading the New Testament, you know that Jesus' disciples weren't exactly Johnnies-on-the-spot. They were just normal, everyday guys.

Which I think is kind of the whole point. Jesus sure did love him some everyday people.

Throughout the New Testament, the only kind of people with whom Jesus consistently takes frightful exception are the very "teachers of the law and Pharisees" whom we see him dressing down in the passages above. One thing that often gets lost in our ideas about Jesus is the degree to which he is *exactly* the wrong person to piss off. And you don't have to spend a lot of time in the New Testament before you understand that the only kind of people who seem to ever truly anger Jesus are those who put religious dogma above what he most clearly stood for, which was God's love.

Around Jesus you can whine, lie, shift your loyalties, be late, be greedy, be too ambitious, be stupid, be a coward, be a hypochondriac, constantly complain, fall asleep at every wrong moment—you can do *nothing* right, and it won't in the slightest way seem to offend him.

But you put dogma ahead of love? You transmogrify God's law into a justification for denying God's love?

Then yikes, man. Then you've got yourself a problem no one in this world wants.

I'm not sure how exactly we came to so often consider Jesus the soft and dreamy, namby-pamby type. But it's hard to believe it came from the accounts of Jesus we have in the Gospels. That's just not the guy on those pages.

Jesus is *scary* when he's riled. And the *only* people who rile him are those who, *in his own name* (what with him being God and all), set themselves up as sanctimonious judges of others.

I think I better go to the weddings of my gay friends. I'm scared *not* to. While it's certainly true that in many of his parables it's unclear what exactly Jesus was saying or meant, he didn't even almost waffle about his "Love your neighbor as yourself." In conjunction with "Love the Lord your God with [everything you've got]," he very explicitly declared that to be *the greatest commandment,* the one upon which hangs "all the law and the prophets."

How in the world am I supposed to argue with *that?* Talk about having *God* eliminate your options.

So I'll attend my gay friends' weddings, in the exact same spirit gay friends of mine once attended my own wedding. And if it happens that in the course of either of my friends' weddings or receptions I find myself wondering if I'm doing the morally correct thing, I'll be sure to remember the first miracle of Jesus' recorded in the Bible. I'll remember what he *did* do.

I'll remember that Jesus turned water into wine.

At a wedding.

What Today's Evangelicals Are Telling Gay People

Once upon a time the evangelical Christian's typical response to homosexuality was that gay people are just messed up straight people who need to become better Christians so that God can stop them from being gay.

The complete failure of the "pray away the gay" movement, however, in conjunction with endless evidence that people are simply born gay, has succeeded in finally tossing that hoary argument onto the ash heap of history. But has that stopped evangelicals from arguing against homosexuality? Of course not. They just needed a new argument, is all.

And they found one. Today the Christian argument against gay people is typically … well, this, taken from an email recently sent me:

> Would you support a serial adulterer who leaves his wife, but is just attracted to other women, because that's who he is and how he was born? How about an alcoholic who just can't help himself? Would you support him as he leaves his wife for alcohol? Would you support a glutton? A man of extreme pride? Why does homosexuality get a pass, and not any other sin?

A person with homosexual desires who resists temptation is exactly the same as a married man who resists temptation to carry on affairs with other women—which is to say, a human being battling the temptation to sin. The most compassionate thing that we could tell someone struggling with homosexuality (or any other sin for that matter) is to keep resisting temptation. Keep battling. Don't give in. This is your badge as a Christian, that you fight temptation.

Now the argument is that a gay person struggling against the temptation to be who they really are is no different from anyone else struggling to resist a "sinful" temptation. Now, in other words, the refrain isn't that gay people should stop being gay. Now it's that they should stop *acting* gay.

Evangelicals are positively enamored of this new argument. If I've heard it once, I've heard it ten thousand times. We all have. You whisper "gay" into the ear of a sleeping evangelical, and there's an excellent chance that he or she will start murmuring in their sleep, "Just like any other sinful temptation. We're all sinners. Must resist temptation."

And putting your brain to sleep before you say that is the very best way to say it, too. Because it's an argument that could only make sense to a brain-dead person. It's just too lame for words.

But lemme try to find some words anyway.

Virtually all sins share a crucial, defining, common quality. Because that quality, which is present in every other imaginable sin, is utterly absent from being or acting gay, insisting upon putting homosexuality into the same category as every other sin—or in the category of sin at all—is like gluing wings on a pig, and insisting that the result belongs in the category of "bird." It doesn't. It can't. It won't. Ever.

Here is that Big Difference between homosexuality and all those other activities generally understood to be "sinful": There is no sin I can commit that, by virtue of my having committed it, renders me incapable of loving or being loved. I can commit murder. I can steal. I can rob. I can drink myself to death. I can do any terrible thing at all, and no one would ever claim that intrinsic to the condition that gave rise to my doing that terrible thing is that I am, by *nature*, unqualified for giving or receiving love.

No one tells the chronic drinker, glutton, adulterer, gambler, or any other kind of sinner that having committed their sin—that being the way they are—means they must stop experiencing love.

Yet living without love is exactly what anti-gay Christians insist upon for gay people.

When you tell a gay person to "resist" being gay, what you are really telling them—what you really *mean*—is for them to be celibate. It's okay for them to be gay; they just can't *live out* their gayness.

What you mean is that you want them to condemn themselves to a life absolutely devoid of the kind of romantic, long-term, emotionally and physically intimate love that all people, Christians included, understand not only as their birthright, but as just about the greatest part of being human.

Be alone, you're demanding. Live alone. Don't hold anyone's hand. Don't snuggle on your couch with anyone. Don't cuddle up with anyone at night before you fall asleep. Don't have anyone at your table to chat with over coffee in the morning.

Don't have or raise children.

Don't get married. Live your whole life without knowing that joy, that sharing, that fulfillment.

Be alone. Live alone. Die alone.

The "sinful temptation" that Christians are forever urging LGBT people to resist is love.

Now isn't that funny, given that love is the *one thing* that Jesus was most clear about wanting his followers to extend to others? It's just so funny it makes you want to laugh till you cry.

Words Do Matter.
Bullying Does Matter.

In September of 2010 I interviewed Charles Robbins, then executive director of The Trevor Project, the leading national organization providing crisis intervention and suicide prevention services to lesbian, gay, bisexual, transgender, and questioning youth.

Before getting to the interview, though, here's a bit of data pertinent to it:

Suicide is the 3rd leading cause of death among young people ages 10 to 24 and accounts for 12.2% of the deaths every year in that age group. (2009, CDC, "10 Leading Causes of Death by Age Group – United States, 2009")

LGB youth are 4 times more likely, and questioning youth are 3 times more likely, to attempt suicide as their straight peers. (2011, CDC, "Sexual Identity, Sex of Sexual Contacts, and Health-Risk Behaviors Among Students in Grades 9-12: Youth Risk Behavior Surveillance")

Suicide attempts by LGB youth and questioning youth are 4 to 6 times more likely to result in injury, poisoning, or overdose that requires treatment from a doctor or nurse, compared to their straight peers. (2011, CDC, "Sexual Identity, Sex of Sexual Contacts, and Health-Risk Behaviors Among Students in Grades 9-12: Youth Risk Behavior Surveillance")

Nearly half of young transgender people have seriously thought about taking their lives, and one quarter report having made a suicide attempt. (2007, Suicide and Life-Threatening Behaviors, Grossman, D'Augelli, "Transgender Youth and Life-Threatening Behaviors")

LGB youth who come from highly rejecting families are 8.4 times as likely to have attempted suicide as LGB peers who reported no or low levels of family rejection. (2009, Family Acceptance Project™ "Family rejection as a predictor of negative health outcomes in white and Latino lesbian, gay, and bisexual young adults")

1 out of 6 students nationwide (grades 9-12) seriously considered suicide in the past year. (2011, CDC, "Youth Risk Behavior Surveillance – United States, 2011")

Suicide attempts are nearly two times higher among Black and Hispanic youth than White youth. (2011, CDC, "Youth Risk Behavior Surveillance – United States, 2011")

Each episode of LGBT victimization, such as physical or verbal harassment or abuse, increases the likelihood of self-harming behavior by 2.5 times on average. (2010, American Journal of Public Health, "Mental health disorders, psychological distress, and suicidality in a diverse sample of lesbian, gay, bisexual, and transgender youths")

Me: Charles, how long have you been with The Trevor Project?
Charles: This is my fourth year.
Me: It must be such emotionally grueling work.
Charles: You know, it's both heartbreaking and heartwarming. It's heartbreaking that the need for Trevor Project's services is so

apparent. The volume of calls we get, the number of letters and emails we get every day from young people desperately reaching out for help, the number of completed suicides we hear about ... all of that is terribly heartbreaking. But what's heartwarming about what we do here is how much support there is out there from people who want to help these kids. So many people really do care, really do want to reach out to these deeply disenfranchised young people. So many people are coming to understand that the fact that LGBTQ are *four times* as likely as their heterosexual peers to complete suicide isn't just a problem. It's an epidemic.

Me: Four times. That's so awful.

Charles: It is. And it's not just because being gay means you have, organic to your nature, an increased desire to self-destruct. Being gay doesn't mean you just show up with an inherent tendency to complete suicide.

Me: Wait—explain why you say "complete suicide," rather than the more common "commit suicide."

Charles: Yes, thank you. We encourage people to say that someone *completed* suicide, because in this context the word "commit" sounds too much like crime-talk: it encourages us to think of the person who takes his or her own life as a perpetrator of a crime, rather than what they are, which is a victim. It's just an outdated use of language that we're trying to help change.

Me: Beautiful. Thanks for the explanation. You were saying that being gay doesn't equal being suicidal.

Charles: Exactly. It doesn't. And yet that's what so many people imply. They take data that conclusively shows the much higher prevalence of completed suicides amongst LBGTQ kids compared to heterosexual kids, and try to use it to "prove" that a predilection toward suicide is a *quality* of being gay. And that's just absurd.

Me: Why do so many teenagers who self-identify as gay attempt or complete suicide?

Charles: Because the *protective factors* in their life just aren't there. They don't have in their lives so much of what keeps young people—*any* person—feeling affirmed and worthwhile. A loving family. Supportive friends. A school environment where bullying isn't tolerated. A network of supportive, caring adults. These are the sort of vital protective factors that have been removed from the lives of so many LGBTQ teens. They're alone; they're ostracized; they're maligned; their very being is constantly getting negated. Of course they're susceptible to taking the terrible, final step. Being gay doesn't make you suicidal. Being picked on, victimized, and constantly devalued makes you suicidal.

Me: The teen years are difficult enough without the extra burden of being different from everyone else.

Charles: Exactly. For so many LGBTQ kids, high school is just an unendurable hell.

Me: What's the one thing you'd most like people to know about LGBTQ teens?

Charles: That words and behaviors matter, that they have real consequences that affect real people. "Sticks and stones will break my bones, but words will never hurt me" is the worst adage ever. It's completely wrong. Words do matter. Bullying does matter. Maybe not once or twice—everybody gets bullied sometimes. But LGBTQ kids get bullied *all the time*. It's a way of life for them. It makes their life unlivable. And so many decide, ultimately, that unlivable is exactly what their life is. So they see no choice but to end it. It's tragic. Trying to prevent them from feeling that way, from taking that irrevocable final step, is what we do here at The Trevor Project.

Me: Is there anything in particular that you'd like to say to my Christian readers?

Charles: I think that the fact that so many young people are so tormented—so ostracized by their family, peers, school, and society in general—that rather than engage and participate in life, they choose to end their life, says a lot about the Christian values that everywhere inform our culture. I think each and every one of us needs to look inside of ourselves, and examine those values for both the good and the harm they're doing. What I would also very much like Christians to know is that being gay isn't a *choice* that anyone makes. It's not a switch you can turn off and on. Gay people were born into creation just like anyone else, and to devalue who they are by insisting God didn't *really* make them as they are is to deny them the right to a rich and loving relationship with God—and that's a terrible, terrible thing to deny anybody. No one should ever use scripture to justify removing another person from the spiritual process. If you're a Christian—as I am—you should look to Christ for how to live and act toward others. And what does the Great Commandment of Jesus say, but that we're all supposed to love our neighbors as we love ourselves? I wish more Christians would remember what Jesus himself told them to do.

What's in Your Wallet?

The reason conservative Christians invariably give for asserting that homosexuality is an egregious sin against God is that the Bible says it's so.

"God said it, I believe it!" is the conservative Christian's credo.

The question that raises in my mind is this: If you're going to look to the Bible generally, and to the words of Jesus specifically, for guidance and direction on how to live your life, then don't you need to very assiduously attend to the actual *words* of Jesus? Especially when he's perfectly clear on a particular issue (which, let's face it, doesn't happen nearly as often as we Christians are wont to pretend that it does)?

If you're trying to live your life in obedience to Christ, then you're all about anything Christ actually *says,* right?

Christ said it; you believe it. If you're a Christian, that's your deal. And if you're a conservative Christian, you most certainly look to Jesus for critical input about anything in your life that's especially important to you.

Like money, for instance. Talk about a core life concern, right? Who doesn't care a *lot* about their money?

Here is what Jesus the Christ said about money:

"Sell your possessions and give to the poor." (Luke 12:33)

"You cannot serve God and Money." (Matthew 6:24)

"Do not store up for yourselves treasures on earth, where moth and rust destroy, and where thieves break in and steal." (Matthew 6:19)

"It is easier for a camel to go through the eye of a needle than for a rich man to enter the kingdom of God." (Luke 18:25)

Nowhere in the Bible is Jesus more clear about anything than he is about money. Talk about slamming shut the door on the wiggle room. And that's not the mortal Paul giving financial advice, either. That's *Jesus* doing that. That's the very God of Gods, being as clear as language allows him to be. Which is very, very clear.

I don't see how it's possible to avoid the conclusion that there is something profoundly wrong with any Christian who is not voluntarily as poor as the proverbial church mouse pointing to the Bible as justification for the condemnation of gay people.

How can any self-respecting Christian take literally what Paul said about homosexuality, and at the same time ignore or seriously waffle on what Jesus Christ himself—who never said *a single word* about homosexuality—said about money?

Shown the Church Door

After my wife Catherine and I had spent six years as members of the very first church home for either of us (I, out of freakin' nowhere, became a Christian when I was thirty-eight years old; a year later Cat was all in), we were asked to sign a document asserting that under no circumstances should any person involved in a same-sex relationship be allowed to hold "any position, of any authority" at that Presbyterian USA church.

We had both been elected deacons of the church—which is how we came to learn that part of becoming a deacon there was signing this document.

I actually thought the head of the Deacons Committee was kidding when she laid the statement before each of us to sign. Cat and I knew the woman. She was a member of the small Bible study group we'd attended for years. We liked her. She was sweet.

"Wouldn't it be funny if there really *was* such a document?" I chortled.

Looking slightly confused, our friend said, "But there is. It's this document right here." As if maybe we'd already forgotten them she nudged the papers a little closer to our side of the table. "You have to sign this."

I looked at Cat. She was already looking at me. Although no one but me would have read it, the message Cat's eyes were sending was, "Yikes! Did our train just stop at Crazy Town?"

Then we both bent to read the document.

Having finished with it, I asked our friend, "Do we *really* have to sign this in order to become deacons? Are you actually not kidding?" I'm a fairly private person. Plus, I'm sane. So I like to keep to a minimum signing my allegiance to extremely clumsily articulated amalgams of reactionary theological proclamations combined with blatantly discriminatory hiring policies.

Ya' know. It's just a general rule I have.

"No, I'm not kidding," she said. "You have to sign it. All our deacons do."

"But ... that doesn't really make sense," I said, since, irrationally, I continue to believe in the powers of rational thought. "Why would we have to sign something like this before we're deemed worthy to serve donuts between services and help pass around the collection plate? That's a little ... *draconian*, don't you think? Actually making someone sign their name to something? Isn't that just a little too Joe McCarthy? You understand how that feels a little extreme, right?"

But, alas, she completely didn't.

"Plus, Cat and I have been members here for six years," I said. "In all that time, I've never once heard anyone associated with this church say a single thing about homosexuality. Never a word about it from the pulpit; never in a meeting; never in a class; never in the bulletin; nothing on the website; never a word about it in our Bible study class. Total silence on this matter. And yet it's a matter so important to the church that you can't become a deacon here unless you sign something specifically about it. Doesn't that seem a little weird to you? If, as a church, we're going to believe in a position about something as strongly as we apparently believe in our position on this issue, shouldn't we, at least every once in a while, say *something* about that belief? If we believe it, we should preach it. People in the congregation have a right to know the rules of the club they're in. It's not right for Cat and me to just now be learning about this, don't you think?"

"Well, I'm sorry that you weren't aware of our position," said our friend who was rapidly seeming like maybe not so much of a friend. "But this is what we believe. And you both have to sign this if you want to become deacons here."

"But we're talking about being *deacons,* right?" piped in Cat. She was then Chief Financial Officer of a major non-profit. Organizational hierarchies are kind of her bag. "It's not like we're being named pastors of the church. We're talking about being *deacons.* Visiting shut-ins. Helping put out chairs at meetings. That sort of thing, right? Nothing that has anything whatsoever to do with who should or shouldn't be hired at the church. Just *deacons,* right?"

Yada, yada, yada, and our choices were exactly two: either sign the "No gay person should be so much as a door greeter or janitor at our church" document—or, by virtue of not signing that document, fail to qualify as deacons of our church.

"Please let us be deacons without signing the paper," we begged the high mucky-mucks of our church (almost all of whom were in our Bible study group). "We love this church. We'd love to help with it. It's not like we're going to be in a position of *hiring* anyone at the church. Isn't it possible to allow us to serve as deacons without our first having to sign that paper?"

Yeah, so that'd be a no.

Thus were Cat and I put in the weird position of being members of a church, the leaders of which had decided—had, in the end, *publicly* decided—that we were not morally suitable to be deacons.

Don't you just *hate* it when you're reduced to the status of second-class citizen in your own church?

I'm joking now, but at the time the whole affair really hurt. It's difficult being told you aren't spiritually qualified to visit people who couldn't make it to church, to help with the services, to greet people at the newcomers' table. All that. We were deemed unfit to do any of it.

And it was *really* difficult when, in the course of our "discernment process," the pastor of our church—a man whom I had every reason to consider a personal friend—placed in the lobby of the church, right beside the doors leading into the sanctuary, stacks of a piece he had previously written about how Christians who don't hold the "correct" view on homosexuality are heretics.

That's the word he used, repeatedly: heretics. And every person at our church knew why he'd put that article out, and to whom it was referring.

Ultimately, Cat and I felt we had no choice but to leave the church that for so long had meant so much to us. Lots of good people there. But in the end (and to a person) they preferred our leaving the church to our serving it without first signing their anti-gay declaration.

Torn from her first church home, Cat cried for days.

Then she did what Cat does best: she started studying the issue of the relationship between the Bible and homosexuality. She basically disappeared into her office for two weeks. When she came out, she was carrying a huge sheaf of papers, which she dropped on the coffee table before me.

"This whole thing about how Christians are supposed to be anti-gay is complete bullshit," she said. "You need to start blogging about this."

An Angel Learns to Judge

Professor Malachi, Dean of Discernment and Judgment at The University of Heaven, tapped a file resting on the middle of his desk. "Let's consider this candidate for heaven right here," he said. "The man is homosexual. Now, what do you think? Should we allow him into heaven?"

The student angel Arthur shifted uncomfortably in his chair. Finally he said, "No, we don't."

"We don't? Are you sure?"

Arthur paused in case he wasn't. He almost desperately wanted to impress Professor Malachi, who had unexpectedly invited him into his office for this chat. "Well, the Bible clearly states that homosexuality is a sin."

"Does it? What's the first thing we teach here about sin, Arthur?"

Arthur remembered his Introduction to Judgment class. "That it's contextual."

"Exactly. When is it *not* a sin to kill?"

"When it's done in the service of a greater good. In defense of the weak. In self-defense. Or even if it's an accident."

"Very good. So despite the fact that the Bible says, 'Thou shalt not kill.'?"

"We consider the context in which any killing has occurred before determining whether or not that killing was a sin."

"Right. And if a woman tells her best friend that the Christmas cookies she made for her were so delicious that she ate them all, even though she really threw them in the garbage because they tasted like dead cat?"

Arthur laughed. "No sin." He recalled his time back on earth, when he told his Grandma how much he loved the bulky purple and green sweater she'd knit him.

"Even though the Bible says very clearly 'Thou shalt not lie'?"

"Even though. Because the larger good was served by her showing affection to her friend."

"And the poor man who steals a loaf of bread from the kitchen of a rich man to feed his starving children?"

"No sin."

"Despite the very clear words of the Bible's Eighth Commandment, 'Thou shalt not steal'?"

"Still no sin. Because there is no judging of sin without first judging that sin's context."

The professor smiled. "We'll make a master angel of you yet, Arthur."

"Thank you, sir." Arthur took a moment to look at the vast shimmering empyrean everywhere around the two of them.

"Quite a sight, isn't it?" said Malachi.

"Even when I dreamed of it on earth, I never imagined anything like it."

"Speaking of those not yet here amongst us. Right off the bat, Arthur, do you vote thumbs up or down for our gay applicant?"

"Well, I know that as a Christian on earth I definitely believed that homosexuality was a sin. That's all I was ever taught."

"You died in your mid-twenties, Arthur. Had you continued to hold that same belief up until the time of your accident?"

"No, I didn't. I mean, not exactly. By then the whole issue had grown more complicated. All I ever heard growing up was that being gay was extremely sinful. I learned that basically there was no such thing as a homosexual: that gay people were really just straight people who needed to get right with God."

"You believed it was possible to, as they say, 'pray away the gay.'"

"I did believe that, yes."

"As did most Christians. Did you continue to believe that?"

"Well, over time it became pretty obvious how wrong that was. It became clear that nobody could just pray away their gay—that some people really *were* just born gay, the same as some people are born left-handed or red-headed."

"Ah. And what was the general Christian teaching after that became the common Christian understanding?"

"Then we were taught that while it might not have been possible for a gay person to stop being gay, it *was* possible for any gay person to resist the temptation to give in to their homosexual tendencies."

"And what exactly does that mean, you think, to 'give into one's homosexual tendencies'?"

"I guess it means to engage in homosexual sex. To actually, physically, *be* gay. I mean, what else could it mean?"

"Nothing that I can see. So the new Christian idea became that gay people could, and should, will themselves to resist being at least physically intimate with others of their kind—to never, in short, have life partners in the way that straight people do. To never marry, for instance."

"Yes. Just like everyone else, they were supposed to resist the sins that they personally were tempted to commit."

"So by that reasoning—the reasoning that all people are sinful and need to resist whatever urges they have to sin—gay people were deemed to be no different from anyone else. Now it was *inherently* no more of a sin to be gay than it was to be straight. All were then understood to start out on the same moral footing. *All* were then innocent, in other words, until proven guilty."

Arthur thought for a moment. "That's right. That's how it was."

"So tell me, where has all this left you on the gay issue?"

"Still a bit confused. I honestly don't know what to make of the whole question of the sinfulness of homosexuality."

"Then let's reason it out, shall we? If I correctly understood you, you no longer hold to the idea that it's a sin *just* to be gay, any more than it's automatically a sin to be, as you said, left-handed, or red-haired—which is to say, any more than it is to be straight. Yes?"

"Yes."

"So a person's sinfulness is no longer determined by what they *are*, but rather solely and exclusively by what they *do*. No manifest sin exists, in other words, before a sinful action is actually committed. Correct?"

"Correct."

"So—and forgive my redundancy; I just want to be absolutely certain we're on the same page—virtually the only way to judge if anyone, gay, straight, or otherwise, has done something sinful, is by evaluating what they actually did. There is simply no other way to determine sinfulness."

"Yes. That does make sense."

"And what do we know to be *the* indispensable tool for judging the morality of any given action?"

"Context."

"Context. Sometimes killing, lying, and stealing is a sin; sometimes it's not. It depends on the context. And when we look to context to determine morality, what two qualities do we look *for?*"

"Harmful intent and harmful action," said Arthur. "At the motives behind the action, and the harm that resulted from the action. Or, as you put it in one of your lectures, *To find the sin, look within.*"

Professor Malachi brought his hand to his heart. "How it touches me to learn that one of my students has listened during class. So, what does our beloved Bible say about the *context* of homosexual sex?"

Arthur thought for a long moment. "The Bible says virtually nothing about any sort of contextual situation relative to homosexuality. It just *lists* homosexuality as a sin. It refers to no context at all."

"Which means that the Bible can, in no way, tell us whether or not any given act of homosexuality is a sin, yes?"

"Yes. It doesn't do that. It can't do that."

"But we *do* know that being a homosexual, in and of itself, is not sinful. We know that we can only judge *acts,* not God-given states of being. And we know that devoid of context, we have nothing upon which to base those judgments, do we?"

"No, we don't."

"Which brings us back to the question of our gay applicant. Do we accept him into heaven, or do we reject his application?"

"Well, I guess I couldn't say. Not at this point, anyway. In order for me to make that call I would first have to know the man— really *know* him—as a person."

"Yes!" cried the professor. "That is exactly right, Arthur! Exactly right. You have reasoned through to the very heart and truth of the matter. And so you will leave this office a wiser and kinder angel than when you entered it, simply because you were willing to do that reasoning. And God bless you for that willingness, son."

A Methodist to
Their Madness

I'll never forget October 15, 2011. That's the day I received in my email this press release:

Methodist Group to Perform Gay Weddings

· In unprecedented move, network of 900+ bypasses denomination's ban to reach out directly to LGBT people

A group of over 900 United Methodists in New York and Connecticut today announced their intention to make weddings available to all people, gay and straight, in spite of their denomination's ban on gay marriage. The announcement marks the kick-off of a project called **We *do*! Methodists Living Marriage Equality**.

In an unprecedented move in any major religious denomination, **We *do*!** is not only bypassing the formal rules of the church, but also reaching out directly to LGBT groups in New York and Connecticut to let them know about the new network. This morning the group published a list of all its members: clergy members who will perform weddings for gay couples, lay members of the denomination who support them, and congregations who have adopted policies to formally make weddings available to all couples.

"We refuse to discriminate against any of God's children and pledge to make marriage equality a lived reality within the New York Annual Conference, regardless of sexual orientation or gender expression," the group declared in statement called A Covenant of Conscience and signed by 164 clergy members, 732 lay people and six entire congregations. In all, 73 congregations within the New York Annual Conference (NYAC) are represented among the signers. NYAC is the regional church body representing United Methodist congregations from Long Island to the Catskills and in southern Connecticut.

"My ordination vows require me minister to all people in my congregation," said Rev. Sara Lamar-Sterling, the minister at First and Summerfield United Methodist Church in New Haven, CT. "This is about pastoral care, about welcoming all people, but especially the marginalized and the oppressed, like Jesus did." Lamar-Sterling and her clergy colleagues are risking their jobs and their careers by taking this stand, but they say their integrity as pastors leaves them no choice but to refuse the church's mandate to discriminate. Over the years, many individual United Methodist clergy have defied the church's ban, but the We do! project marks the first time an organized network of clergy has done so, and done so with the support of many hundreds of lay members of the church.

"The recognition of the full humanity, sacred worth, and equal rights of gay and lesbian people is crucial to the civil rights struggle of our time. Gay, lesbian, and straight United Methodist laity and clergy are caught in an inescapable network of mutuality, tied in a single garment of destiny," the Covenant of Conscience states, citing Martin Luther King's famous Letter from Birmingham Jail. "The continuing denial of full access to all the rights and privileges of church membership in the United Methodist Church is causing deep spiritual harm to our gay and lesbian brothers and sisters and is a threat to us all."

The United Methodist Church *Book of Discipline*, the rulebook that governs the country's third largest Christian denomination, states "Ceremonies that celebrate homosexual unions shall not be conducted by our ministers and shall not be conducted in our churches." It is one of several anti-gay provisions of the church, which since 1972 has declared "the practice of homosexuality is incompatible with Christian teaching." The church General Conference meets quadrennially to revise the *Discipline* and the issue of LGBT exclusion has been hotly debated at each General Conference in the last 40 years.

The **We** *do!* project has been over a year in the making and has been followed by similar efforts in 11 other conferences within the UMC. All told, over 1,000 clergy in 19 states and the District of Columbia have signed a pledge vowing to extend their ministry to all couples seeking the church's blessing for their relationships. The growing pastoral movement has caused a stir within the church and is expected to have reverberations at the upcoming General Conference.

We *do!* **Methodists Living Marriage Equality** is sponsored by Methodists in New Directions (MIND), a grassroots organization working in the New York Annual Conference of the UMC dedicated to ending the church's prejudice and discrimination against LGBT people. It is co-sponsored by the NY Chapter of the Methodist Federation for Social Action (MFSA), an organization bringing people together to work for peace and justice in the church and the world. Both organizations are independent of the United Methodist Church. More information on the initiative is available on the MIND website.

"What a *story!*" I thought excitedly. "I must snag an interview with this Reverend Sara Lamar-Sterling!"

My heart quickened at the thought of probing into the mind of this renegade Christian leader, this bold iconoclast, this trailblazing visionary who was willing to defy authority, buck convention, and let the chips fall where they may.

Every journalist dreams of the day when a cutting-edge, paradigm-busting, career-making story falls right into their lap.

And that day had just arrived for me.

One hour later I was still strategizing about how to use my extensive network of media contacts to land an interview with Rev. Lamar-Sterling. Then I realized that I could just pick up the phone and call the number on the press release.

"Would you like to talk to Sara?" said the friendly lady on the other end of the line. "I can give you her cell number if you want. Do you have a pen and paper?"

Did *I* have a pen and paper? Was she serious? Was she not aware that I am the *ultimate* crack reporter? It was like asking Superman if he has a cape.

Moments later I had the fiery dissenter herself on the phone. I steadied myself. This was it. History was calling, and I was poised to take its message.

Now, I like to begin my interviews with high-profile, controversial social mavericks by zinging at them a question that shoots directly into the very heart of the issue at hand. Sure, some see my hard-hitting, uncompromising interview style as abrasive, even bare-knuckles brutal. And I'm not gonna lie about it: my direct, in-your-face questions cause a lot of would-be media darlings to crumble like a mummy's cookie.

But you know what those questions get me that a lot of those starry-eyed "reporters" *don't* get with their namby-pamby questions? Real answers, that's what. Answers from the heart. Answers from the gut.

Sure, a lot of time those answers come through tears. But, hey: if you can't take the heat, don't stand in the spotlight. That's my motto.

By way of unleashing my first jaw-dropping uppercut, I said to Rev. Lamar-Sterling, "So, are you bummed about probably having to spend all of eternity in hell?"

The reverend burst out with a laugh so hearty the phone almost fell out of my hand. Once the major swell of her hilarity had subsided, she said, "Oh, that was a good one! No, no, I'm not worried about anything like that. Hell is a creative idea dreamed up by Dante and his friends."

Oh. Well. Okay. Not exactly how I'd expected that to go. Still: pretty edgy thing to say!

She sure did sound *nice*. Which, I knew, could mean only one thing: she was a pro, a veteran of the PR wars who knew a thing or two about artfully manipulating the media. But I wasn't just any fawning TV-show host come to lob softballs a toddler could knock out of the park.

"Are you afraid that for taking the stand you have," I asked, "you might *lose your job?*" Boom. Shot fired, right on target. I couldn't wait to watch her squirm.

"Lose my *job?*" said Lamar-Sterling cheerily. "For doing *this?* No, that's not a concern. There are many steps that would have to happen in order for any of us involved in this to actually lose our positions within the church."

Wow. There was really no getting around it: a lesser reporter than I would have found her apparently unflagging good cheer a tad challenging.

"But that *could* happen, right?" I asked, with an air of conspiratorial subterfuge that I hoped she might find contagious. "You *could* lose your job, couldn't you?" I imagined her in tattered clerical robes, walking the mean streets of New Haven, CT, sadly holding out to passers-by a battered brass collection plate.

"Well, I suppose losing my job is in the realm of possibilities," she said. "But it's not anything I'm afraid of. In any account, the much bigger picture, for we who have come out in favor of marriage equality, is the fact that gay and lesbian people are excluded and discriminated against every single day of their lives. That's what really matters here. *They're* the ones really bearing a risk out in the world. Compared to theirs, our daily risk is much smaller."

That was it.

I gave up. This woman was clearly the greatest pastor in the history of niceness.

In my final effort to inject into this story at least *some* grit, I said, "Did you have to put together this movement in secret?" *Sneaky priest, featured piece* is an old adage of journalism. Probably. Somewhere.

"In secret? Gosh, no. We've been openly working on this for years. We've always been very open about talking about this, and about sharing our purposes and goals, and collecting signatures and so on. It's all been very above-board. A great many people within the Methodist church believe in marriage equality, and so we've just been honored to facilitate and advance that conversation. And through initiatives like 'We *do!*', we look forward to doing a great deal more of this in the future."

"How did your own church react to your doing this?" I asked. I pictured the congregants of her church up on their feet, screaming, railing, gnashing their teeth, brandishing rolled-up church bulletins they'd fashioned into short-lived but menacing torches.

"Oh, they *love* it. They're a reconciling congregation, so they've been very excited about the whole project. In fact, I actually had to slow them down a bit. I had to explain to them how this is a process, how we needed to work within the larger body of the New York Annual Conference, to bring everyone along at the same time. But they've been absolutely supportive of this every step of the way."

I asked Rev. Lamar-Sterling about where the "We *do!*" movement fits within the larger body of Methodists. So she explained to me how there are different "conferences," or regions, of Methodists, across the country, and how each, reflecting the sensibilities of its citizens, is necessarily dealing with the issue of marriage equality in its own way, and at its own speed.

"The same sort of thing we're doing here in the NYAC is currently going on in eleven other Methodist conferences," she said. "The difference is that while their efforts are geared toward clergy only, 'We *do!*' involves clergy, laity, and congregations. That's what makes what we're doing so exciting. 'We *do!*' is a strong collective of faithful Christians people who have come together to affirm that a gay and lesbian couple have as much right to the sacred bond of holy matrimony as anyone else."

She then explained about how *The Book of Discipline*, which constitutes the law and doctrine of the United Methodist Church, is a living document, and not, as she put it, "a baseball bat for hurting others," and how every four years (starting in 1784!) representatives of all the Methodists get together, talk about what's *in The Book of Discipline*, make whatever changes or adjustments to its text are voted necessary, and then publish a new edition of the *Book.*

Boy, these guys really put the *organized* in organized religion. It's all so ... well, extremely democratic.

(Fact break: In the United States, The United Methodist Church ranks as the largest mainline denomination, the second largest Protestant church after the Southern Baptist Convention, and the third largest Christian denomination. As of 2007, worldwide membership was about 12 million: 8.0 million in the United States and Canada, 3.5 million in Africa, Asia and Europe. So. There's that.)

"Ultimately, I and others who believe in the sanctity of marriage equality would like the language of *The Book of Discipline* to be changed to reflect full affirmation of gay and lesbian equality," said the reverend. "But will those changes be made this year, or next? They very well might. But either way, it will ultimately happen. I'm confident that Christ will guide the United Methodist Church to become the welcoming, just, and reconciling church it was meant to be."

I asked if there was anything final she'd care to say.

"I would like everyone to know that all people are created in God's image; all are sacred," she said. "God's love is not discriminatory, or selective; it does not include some, and exclude others. It is for all. I want gay and lesbian people to know that they are welcomed in the United Methodist Church. Come, join us, as we, along with you, say, we *do!*"

As I later reflected back on my conversation with the good reverend, I fell asleep. I dreamed I was a Jimmy Olsen-style reporter, pitching the story of the "We *do!*" movement to the editor of a big New York newspaper.

"*Over nine hundred!*" I told him. "That's a lot of Methodists!"

The man who had probably been called "Chief" since he was in diapers was sitting on a leather high-backed chair behind a wooden desk you could land a helicopter on. He wore his usual outfit: gray slacks held up by suspenders over one of the white shirts he must have bought with the sleeves rolled up. The old man was cantankerous, sure, his edges so rough you could practically use the air around him to sand wood. But dammit, he was fair. And he knew the business inside out. The man had ink flowing through his veins.

"Look, kid," said the Chief, speaking around his well-chomped cigar. "I'm not saying this is no story at all. But it isn't exactly a five-ton reptile stomping down the middle of Broadway, is it? What you have here is a bunch of Christians who looked into their hearts, found God telling them that gay people have the same right to have their relationships blessed by Him as straight people do, who then organized themselves into a group that reflects that belief. That's what's happened here, right, kid?"

"Well, yeah, it is, basically."

"I got news for ya, son: that ain't news. That's Methodists being *methodical*. What you have is a story about *meetings*. It's a story about schedules, procedures, conferences, rules of order. It's about purposeful conversation, intentional reflection, collective discernment. It's about that vast, invisible matrix of undulating forces that, slowly but surely, has always worked to evolve the body of Christ on earth."

Suddenly the Chief was transformed into a radiant figure emanating a bright golden light that filled the room.

"Who *are* you?" I whispered.

Spreading his (or her?) arms wide as it expanded, rose in the air, and became too bright for me look directly at, the figure said, "I am the Lord your God. The story of gay people and my church is still being written. Pity those too blind to see how happily that story must end, how inevitably all will know that I created and equally love gay people, straight people, and everyone in between."

As suddenly as it had appeared the figure and its light vanished, replaced by the Chief once again sitting behind his desk.

"Now get out there and find me a story I can use," he said. Bending over the papers on his desk, he grumbled, "Extra points if it involves a live dinosaur."

Our Devastated Mountaintop

"If you're not with us you're against us."

"What you call the 'middle ground' I call a sinkhole."

"You wouldn't know the Bible from a Hello Kitty autograph book, you insufferably sanctimonious simp."

Okay, I never said that last one. Or the other two, actually. But I know they all sound like things I *might* have said.

For when it comes to Certain Causes, I know I can seem like a bit of a maniac.

And by "Certain Causes," I think we all know what I mean. That's right: creative capitalization.

I'm so *tired* of not being able to capitalize whatever words I want. *No More!*

No, but seriously: I write quite a bit about the relationship between gay people and Christianity.

So here's the thing: I don't particularly *love* writing on that issue. I don't do it because I think it's cool, or attention-getting, or enjoy having rabid fundies buzz my site like fume-spewing Nazi Luftwaffters.

I write on that matter for one reason, and one reason only: I love Christianity. *Love it.* Christianity is the most awesome thing to happen to mankind since a few mutant chimps exclaimed, "Whoa, check us out. Thumbs!"

There is no question of the mind or soul for which Christianity does not provide an outstanding answer. In the figure of Jesus Christ is found everything real and important that God wants communicated to man. Christ is the final proof of the depth of God's love for us. Christianity is unutterably sublime, enthrallingly mystical, and philosophically complete. It's perfect.

But *people* have so thoroughly trashed it that at this point Christianity is like the site of a mountaintop removal. Its whole crown has been so perniciously razed that its organic, abounding, life-supporting beauty is all but gone. What was majestically inspiring has been reduced to nothing so much as an appalling testament to man's selfishness and arrogance.

I don't write about gay people because I love them so much. I don't love gay people any more than I do anyone else. They're just *people*. But they're an entire *class* of people who are every day being cruelly maligned, denigrated, bullied to death, and in every way dehumanized—by *Christians*. People representing the faith to which *I* ascribe are, in the name of that faith, purposefully, consciously, and even gleefully tending to the destruction of people whose only "crime" is that they love in a way that's *barely* different from the way the majority of people love.

How can I live with that? How am I supposed to be okay with that? It's so wrong. It's so hideous. It's so inexcusable. It's the crudest, most damaging kind of transgression.

It needs to stop.

And as surely as one day follows the next, sooner or later it will stop.

First we got rid of the atrocious idea that the Bible justifies slavery. Then we (*cough*mostly*cough*) got rid of the idea that the Bible justifies the subjugation of women. And before long this final, ugly wall will also come tumbling down.

Writing on the gay issue is how I swing my pen-shaped sledgehammer against that wall.

I, my friends on this site, and increasing numbers of Christians every day aren't fighting against anything, so much as we're fighting *for* something.

We're fighting for what we know Christianity could and should be.·

Can you imagine what Christianity would be if it weren't for the reprehensible anti-gay nonsense that clings to it like dog mess you can't get off your shoe? Can you imagine if Christianity wasn't so easy to associate with ignorance and bigotry? Can you imagine a Christianity that immediately sparks thoughts of honor, respect, inspiration, compassion, patience, and joy?

Can you imagine a Christianity that evokes the light of love, instead of the darkness that is love's opposite?

I can. And if you can, too, then together we can usher onto center stage this new Christianity, and relegate to the wings the posturing, bellowing, utterly unconvincing old Christianity that for much too long now has been hogging the spotlight.

I'm not obsessed with the gay issue. What I am obsessed with is restoring that glorious mountaintop to its natural state.

Can a Man Act Too Effeminate?

On my blog I often answer questions readers send me. Here's one such letter, followed by my answer to it:

Hi John,

Just read your blog posts on homosexuality—very insightful. I am a homosexual man myself. However, I am extremely effeminate (not to the point of transgenderism), and I was wondering: What are your thoughts on males who behave like females (wearing make-up, into fashion, etc.)?

Sometimes, I feel that God does not like the way I am. So would you say I should change even though this comes naturally for me? Thanks so much! I greatly would appreciate your response and time taken to write it. God bless.

The only reason I'd suggest changing is if *not* changing is bringing you too much pain, trouble or grief. If you're getting *beaten up* every day for wearing make-up, I'd advise you to quit wearing make-up. I'm no conformist; but I'm also pretty down with surviving. I want you to be okay. If being okay means you have to tweak a little of what you do here and there, then … then that's life. We all do that. What's natural for me, for instance, is to be naked while I clean my house. But I stopped doing that, when a traumatic accident caused me to learn that cleaning the house naked can lead to one of the weirdest ways *ever* to ruin a perfectly good vacuum cleaner.

But this isn't about me. It's about you, thank God.

The above caveat being said: no, I don't think you should change. Screw changing. Be the way you are. It's *good* for us to have men who act like (stereotypical) women, and women who act like (stereotypical) men. Because those are the kind of people who are leading the way for all of us to be *exactly who we really are*. People like you are the heroes of our culture.

I'm a six-foot-two, 215-pound man who's about one nanoliter of testosterone away from being a werewolf. If I were any straighter I could hire myself out as a T-square. Well, I *love* Broadway musicals. I'm *completely* interested in women's fashions. And not just because of the women who wear them; I'm enamored with the whole idea of fashion as art. When talking I move my hands around so much it's like they're secretly trying to message for help.

I hate the thought of acting like the term "March Madness" triggers in me any thought at all beyond "Everyone's horny in the spring." Though I'm awesome at all sports, the one I chose to focus on was tennis, which nine out ten sports enthusiasts agree ranks on the Gay-o-Meter just below synchronized swimming. And in high school I *quit* the tennis team so I could *act in the school plays*. (My athlete friends to me: "Don't you think acting is a little *gay*?" Me to them: "Well, let's see. I spend my time surrounded by straight alpha girls who know they're pretty enough to be actresses. You spend your time chasing and climbing all over other guys, and then taking showers with them. But *I'm* gay?")

I'm a child of the fifties. My father's generation of men was stuck doing nothing but working like mad men and as much as possible distancing themselves from their emotions. While in high school my wife, along with all of her classmates, was given an aptitude test. The boys' test was printed on blue paper; the girls' was on pink.

According to the test, the *only* jobs suitable for young women were nurse, secretary, and teacher. That's it. Those were their three choices.

When I was seventeen years old, a group of gay actors and dancers, slightly older than I and infinitely more sophisticated, took me under their wing. At the time I had zero concept of the whole idea of homosexuality; to me, everyone was ... well, straight like me. The people in the group who took my lost and sorry ass in were *seriously* effeminate men. They giggled; they tittered; they swooned; they faux-fainted; they screamed when to me a simple wide-eyed gasp would have done the trick; while talking they gesticulated so wildly that I learned to step back when they started telling a story. And they did all this in public. They *especially* did it in public. They *liked* being the center of attention. They *wanted* other people to very much register their presence.

They weren't in the least afraid of being who they were.

Those guys *saved* me. By so boldly and uncompromisingly being themselves, they showed me how I, too, could be myself. They proved to me that I didn't have to partition myself into parts, some of which I could show publicly, some of which I couldn't. Because of them I got to bring to the table all of myself, all of the time.

I am every day grateful to those guys (and to their/our female friends who loved them). I don't know what my life would have become without their modeling for me what *whole* people look like. They dared to be different, and in so doing empowered me to do the same.

So, no: unless you must for your own safety, don't change. I don't know a lot about a lot, but I *guarantee* you that God is more than okay with you being the entirety of the person you are—which is to say the entirety of the person God created you to be. You're a guy who's inclined to behave in ways most people associate with women. Lots of men are like that. Lots of women like to behave in ways most people consider masculine.

It's all good. It's more than good; it's important. Because *all* of us are right now in the process of learning the one thing that, come hell or high water, we all certainly will learn, which is that ultimately no behavior, thought process, or natural inclination is exclusively male or female. We all contain a great deal of both. And it's thanks to people like you—people who were essentially born to be trailblazers—that we're all becoming more and more comfortable embracing that divine truth.

The Illusion of the Middle Ground

In recent years some Christian leaders have responded to the gay issue by making a ministry of "building bridges" between those who believe that being gay is a sin and those who don't. These pastors and ministry leaders make a point of never committing on the matter either way. Instead, as one ministry leader typical of the sort puts it, "we create stepping stones from one end of the spectrum to the other, establishing a neutral, non-judgmental, values-free middle ground, where parties on either side of the gay-Christian debate can meet to together discuss and explore the issue."

And I certainly understand how great that sounds.

But it's not great. It doesn't even make sense. Because when it comes to the issue of LGBT equality, there is no middle ground. There can't be. The Christian/LGBT issue is a *moral* issue. And moral issues are by definition about right and wrong.

And this particular moral issue is one of no small consequence. There couldn't be more at stake with it. The Christians on one side of this debate are claiming that, in the eyes of God, those on the other side are *less than human.*

Whoosh. Good-bye middle ground.

No matter how strenuously he or she might deny it, any Christian who fails to forthrightly and unambiguously assert that there is nothing whatsoever inherently immoral about same-sex relationships *has* chosen a side in this conflict. They've chosen to perpetuate the maligning, ostracizing, and degradation of gay people by Christians. If you don't stop one person from abusing another, of what good are you to the victim? To a starving man, the person who can't decide whether or not they want to share their food is no better than the person who outright refuses to.

I'm all for conversations about critical moral issues. And of course in every last way I encourage people on opposite sides of this issue to reach out to one another; I must spend a fourth of my life carefully and thoughtfully engaging with Christians whose theology on homosexuality is radically different from mine. But in order for such conversations to be of any genuine value, they must be intentional. They must explicitly have resolution as their purpose. A bridge that goes nowhere, or stepping stones that quickly circle back to their starting point, are useless.

When it comes to weighty moral issues, there's nothing wrong with traveling across the middle ground. But it's at best folly and at worse a harmful lie to maintain that it's morally feasible to remain in that middle ground. No one wanders the desert forever.

It's true that on the issue of LGBT and Christian relations I am impatient. But I'm impatient for a good reason. Christian leaders on the right do not hesitate to loudly and boldly claim their moral certitude. From the left-hand channel of that stereo, however, we too rarely hear anything but silence or static. It's time for the left to dial in its station, switch from "mono" to "stereo," turn up the volume, and start broadcasting the message that it's perfectly okay to be gay.

Christian leaders who persist in doing nothing more than "elevating the conversation" succeed in doing nothing more than alleviating the pangs of conscience that Christians on the right should be encouraged to feel for clinging to their convictions that same-sex relationships are an abomination before God. Instead of evading their moral responsibility, "progressive" Christians need to once and for all, forthrightly and unequivocally, proclaim their full and unconditional acceptance of same-sex relationships. They need to do that for the sake of gay people, and for the sake of the millions who have lost their faith in God because they cannot reconcile the gross disparity between a clear moral precept and the only thing they ever hear Christian leaders actually say.

Hello, Jesus

The rational Christian must admit that no one actually, in an objective sense, *knows* if there's a hell, or *knows* how God feels about homosexuality. Any of us can pretend that we know those things, of course. But none of us really does. The Bible is open to an infinite number of perfectly legitimate interpretations. That's one of its great miracles: in so many ways, and about so many things, the Bible insists that ultimately we must arrive at our own understandings and conclusions.

If the Bible were perfectly and explicitly clear on where God stands on the issues of hell and LGBT people, today the question of homosexuality would not be dividing Christendom in two, and great numbers of Christians would not be taking seriously the idea that nothing in the New Testament is meant to indicate that hell is a real and literal place.

The bottom line is that each Christian has to decide for him or herself whether there's a hell, and whether God is or isn't okay with people being and living gay.

When God comes to earth, and walks and talks as a man, you can be sure that, right off the bat, you're into a whole bunch of stuff you will never, ever fathom. But as confoundingly complex as the Bible is, the one thing within it that comes across with extreme clarity is that Jesus' primary, fundamental mission and purpose was one of love. The *one* thing in the Bible that's crystal clear is that Jesus came to help us grasp the fullness and magnitude of God's love for us.

This is my take on Jesus, anyway: first and foremost he meant to communicate the infinite degree to which each of us, individually, is loved by God.

Once I accept that as true, I know *exactly* what to make of the "controversial" questions of gay people and hell. If you begin with the conviction that (as 1 John 4:8 tells us), God is love, and you take seriously Jesus' declaration that one-half of the *most important of all laws* is that we love our neighbors, then the debate over whether God does or doesn't send all non-Christians to hell, or whether God is okay with gay people being gay, dissolves. Because thinking and talking about hell and/or God's condemnation of gay people moves you beyond what you *know* to be true about Jesus Christ, and into what can only amount to speculation about him.

I'm a slow-witted person. I don't like to think too much. I prefer to go with what I know, and, where possible, to shed the rest.

The idea of a God who would condemn to hell forever all non-Christians and gay people is logically, diametrically opposed to the idea of a God who loves mankind. It would mean that God is not obeying the very law about which he himself, as Jesus, declared none greater.

It would mean God *breaking* his own Great Commandment!

That just doesn't make sense.

So I reject it.

I start with the love of Jesus; I let everything else fall away.

Good-bye hell.

Good-bye the idea that "gay Christian" is an oxymoron.

Hello, Jesus.

Their Hall of Mirrors

Every Christian who believes that homosexuality is an abominable sin against God invariably points to the Bible as justification for this belief. What else can they do but that? Such a person isn't about to blame themselves for their prejudice. The Bible is all they have: there exists no other "proof" that gay people, just by *being* gay, offend God. Challenge a Christian to make one single argument for homosexuality being wrong that does not quote or reference the Bible, and suddenly they're in a house of mirrors; suddenly, the only thing they can point to is themselves.

So they'll only close their eyes, and scream into their self-created darkness, "It doesn't matter! Because the Bible *does* condemn homosexuality!"

They're flat wrong about that; the Bible doesn't condemn homosexuality. (For more on that, see this book's opening chapter, *Taking God at His Word: The Bible and Homosexuality.*)

So let's instead talk to our imaginary anti-gay Christian about the one thing that we know he or she most cares most about in the whole world: Jesus Christ.

And when we read the Gospels, what do we find to be the primary quality of Jesus Christ? Compassion. Jesus cared for nothing so much as he did relieving the suffering of others. Relieving the suffering of others is what Jesus came to do. That was his mission. That's what he was *here* for.

One of the most famous incidences of Jesus relieving the suffering of another is the story, told in John 5, of the time he healed a man who for thirty-eight whole years had been a cripple:

> Then Jesus said to him, "Get up! Pick up your mat and walk." At once the man was cured; he picked up his mat and walked.

On the scene at the time were some Jewish religious leaders. They responded to Jesus' miraculous healing of the man by *objecting* to it.

Why? Did they really have so little compassion that they actually preferred for the poor man to *remain* a cripple?

No. What they were so outraged about was that Jesus had disobeyed the Bible. And not in any small way, either. In healing the man, Jesus had violated number eight of the Ten Commandments: he had worked on the Sabbath. ("*Remember the Sabbath day by keeping it holy ... on it you shall not do any work.*")

The religious leaders found Jesus' disregard for the letter of the law an offense too egregious for them to abide. And they were deadly serious about that:

> So because Jesus was doing these things on the Sabbath, the Jewish leaders began to persecute him.

Persecute him. Because he didn't wait until *the next day* to heal the crippled man.

So let's recap, shall we?

When faced with suffering, Jesus did not hesitate; he did not prevaricate; he did not obfuscate. He acted. He was perfectly aware that in alleviating the lame man's suffering he was breaking a primary, explicit command of the Bible. But he didn't care. He did it anyway.

Jesus chose compassion over legalism.

He ignored one of the most significant and weighty laws of the Bible, because it interfered with him doing the right thing.

Again: *Jesus chose compassion over legalism.*

Thus do we learn that any Christian who chooses to obey the letter of the Bible's law over extending compassion to another is utterly and blatantly failing Christ by failing to follow Christ's example.

Gay people are suffering, and have always suffered, because legalistic Christians use the Bible as justification for at best treating them like second-class citizens, and at worst viciously persecuting them. Such Christians fail to emulate God by ignoring the example of His only begotten son.

The response of the dedicatedly legalistic Christian to this clear and simple reasoning is as predictable as it is inevitable. He or she will claim that just as the lame man whom Jesus healed was physically sick, so the gay person is spiritually sick.

"See?" they will say, "Both need Jesus to heal them!"

Which I suppose sounds reasonable enough. Except for one thing: it ignores the fact that there is something objectively wrong with the lame man, whereas there's nothing whatsoever objectively wrong with the gay person beyond what the Christian uses his Bible to claim there is.

But when we turn to our legalistic Christian in hopes of a response to that point, we will find that he or she, having made their argument, has disappeared back inside their hallowed hall of mirrors, where they will spend countless hours rapturously gazing at grossly distorted images of themselves, all the while mistaking them for God.

World War Gay Has Ended

Unaware that their cause had been lost, a small number of Japanese soldiers deep in the jungles of the Philippines continued waging guerrilla warfare against an imaginary enemy years after World War II had ended.

Via pamphlets dropped from airplanes, newspapers left for them everywhere, and even relatives at the jungle's edges hollering at them through bullhorns, the diehard soldiers *got* the news that the war had ended. They just didn't believe it.

It's now as obvious as a full bright rainbow in a dark gray sky that at most within a couple of generations (if not, at the rate we're going, within a couple of years) any church or denomination still fighting against the marriage of gay couples and the ordination of gay clergy will be like those recalcitrant Japanese soldiers living amongst the mangrove trees of Lubang Island long after everyone else has accepted peace as a fact and adjusted to the new world order. As surely as the complete cessation of gunfire and your cousin's voice through a bullhorn yelling, "Come out! It's over! Stop embarrassing your family!" means that the war you were fighting has ended, gay people will ere long be fully welcomed into every Christian church, where just as many as you please will be serving as pastor and priest.

It took longer for some Christians than it did for others to understand that the Bible does not, in fact, support denying black people their civil rights.

It took longer for some Christians than it did for others to understand that the Bible does not, in fact, support denying women their civil rights.

And now it's taking longer for some Christians than it is for others to understand that the Bible does not, in fact, support denying gay people either their civil or religious rights.

The Presbyterian Church (PCUSA), the Episcopal Church, the Evangelical Lutheran Church, and the United Church of Christ, among an increasing number of other denominations or groupings within them, now favor the ordination of gay and lesbian clergy.

Science continues to affirm homosexuality as inborn (not that anyone who's ever actually known a gay person doubts it).

The Biblical scholarship supporting the idea that Paul never wrote a word proscribing natural homosexuality is at least, if not more, credible and persuasive as the scholarship claiming that he did.

A Gallup Poll done in 1996 showed that 68 percent of Americans were opposed same-sex marriage. By 2012 that number had dropped to 48 percent.

Across the board young people today—including Christians of every denomination—fail to understand why the church makes such a big deal, or any deal at all, about gays and lesbians. In a Gallup Poll conducted in November 2012, 73 percent of people between 18 and 29 years old said they supported same-sex marriage; only four years before it had been 39 percent for and 52 percent against.

The bottom line on the whole LGBT-Christianity issue is that within what historically is an astonishingly short period of time (yay Internet!), we have reached Ye Olde Tipping Point. And from this point on that seesaw will only continue tipping further to the left.

That certainly works for me personally. For verily am I just ever so slightly weary of hollering into the jungle for the deeply confused, bizarrely obdurate Christian combatants in there to stop fighting, lay down their weapons, and come step out into the open, where they can enjoy the sunshine and fresh air, relax, get a hug or ten, and finally be at peace with a whole class of citizens who, from the very beginning, never meant them any harm at all.

Christians and the Blood of Jamey Rodemeyer

Jamey Rodemeyer was a 14-year-old kid from Buffalo, NY, who, in September of 2011, after years of being bullied for being gay, committed suicide.

If you're a Christian who believes that being gay is a morally reprehensible offense against God, then it's critical that you understand that you share a mindset, worldview, and moral structure with the kids who hounded Jamey Rodemeyer, literally, to death. It is your ethos, your convictions, and your theology that informed, supported, and encouraged their cruelty.

We Christians who believe that God created gay people as much in His own image as He did straight people are *begging* you to reconsider your theology—to do nothing more than be open to an alternative, fully credible, *scholastically sound* interpretation of two or three lines from Paul.

On what possible grounds could you refuse to do something so simple, when you see the horrible ultimate cost of that refusal?

Christ died so that you could love more. But instead of evincing love, you now support and willingly participate in a system that allows that same Christ to be used as a moral justification for the most vile kind of abuse.

How could that have happened? How could something so right have gone so wrong?

Turn, friend. And when you do, open your arms. Discover waiting to embrace you a new Christ behind the relative shell of the one you inherited. Jesus Christ died for your sins. That was unthinkably beautiful. Jamey Rodemeyer died *from* your sins. That is not. That is the very hell that, awfully enough, you've somehow tricked yourself into believing your life refutes.

Three days after publishing the above on my blog, I posted an animated short that I wrote and created via the free tools available at xtranormal.com. In the short, entitled, *Christians and Gay Teen Suicides: "How Could Anyone Be So Stupid?"*, two Christians are talking.

Christian One: Hello, my fellow Christian.

Christian Two: Hello there!

Christian One: Isn't it wonderful to be a Christian?

Christian Two: It certainly is.

Christian One: Did you hear about that kid who committed suicide?

Christian Two: The gay teenager?

Christian One: Yes.

Christian Two: I heard about that, yes. What a tragedy.

Christian One: So sad.

Christian Two: Have you been reading in all the blogs how people are saying that we Christians are in some way responsible for the suicide of teenage gays?

Christian One: Why would anyone say something so stupid?

Christian Two: I don't know. Something about how we Christians share the same morality as kids who bullied those poor kids to death.

Christian One: That is crazy. I've never bullied anyone in my life. Have you?

Christian Two: No. That wouldn't be Christian. I'm a good Christian.

Christian One: Me, too. It is absurd for anyone to claim that Christians support the bullying of gay teenagers. I don't want any teenager, gay or otherwise, to be bullied.

Christian Two: Me neither. [Pause.] I *do* want them to stop being gay, though.

Christian One: Well, of course. Being gay is a sin against God.

Christian Two: It sure is.

Christian One: Gay people go to hell.

Christian Two: Yes. That's where gay people are punished for being gay.

Christian One: Yes. It is God's law that gay people be punished.

Christian Two: Being gay is an evil abomination, a moral offense against God.

Christian One: No doubt about that.

Christian Two: Amen.

Christian One: Amen.

Christian Two: Anyway, can you believe those people saying that we good Christians share a worldview, and a moral structure, with the same kids who bullied that poor boy so much he killed himself?

Christian One: I can't believe anyone would actually say that.

Christian Two: Me neither. How could anyone be so stupid?

Christian One: So blind.

Christian Two: So ignorant.

Christian One: So hurtful.

Christian Two: I guess some people just care more about being right than they do about the feelings of others.

Christian One: It is too bad about that teenage boy, though.

Christian Two: It is. What a tragedy.

Christian One: I wonder how something like that could have happened? What were those bullies thinking?

Christian Two: I cannot imagine.

Christian One: Me neither. Oh, well. See you in church this Sunday.

Christian Two: You bet. God bless you.

Christian One: And God bless you.

Christian Two: [Pause.] Um.

Christian One: What is it?

Christian Two: You don't think …

Christian One: What?

Christian Two: That we … that is, I mean, that we, that we, along with the bullies … Do you think maybe—?

Christian One: No, I don't think.

Christian Two: Right. Me neither. I don't know what came over me. See you in church.

Christian One: See you in church.

(Off-screen we hear, first at a distance and then growing louder before fading again, the sound of an ambulance siren.)

An Open Apology from Christians to Gay People

Last night I dreamed that I was standing in the sanctuary of an immense empty cathedral. Broad beams of jewel-colored light cut through the air high above me, coming to illuminate a majestic pulpit that seemed halfway to heaven. Torn between curiosity and trepidation, I made my way up the many stairs leading to the great platform. Before taking the final step onto it I paused; elevated above the pews is no place for me. Where the pastor would set the text of his sermon I saw a sheaf of papers that seemed to draw me forward. When I reached them I read, neatly printed by hand, these words:

To All Gay Persons:

We write you from down upon our knees, our hearts so filled with contrition they are like stones whose weight we cannot bear.

For a grievously long time we have treated gay people in a way that we now understand brings nothing but shame upon the God we purport to emulate. With bilious fury have we systematically maligned, denigrated, condemned, cursed, shamed, and bullied you literally to death.

For no reason beyond animal ignorance we have tried to obliterate you: to rob you of your identity, crush your self-worth, destroy your hopes, turn you against yourselves. We have harnessed our almost unimaginable power to bring to you the singular, unceasing message that God finds you reprehensible.

Shamefully, we have turned the way you love into the way we hate.

And for that we now know that it is we, and not you, who deserve hell.

Over and again we have asked ourselves how we could have been so wrong. How, in the name of a loving God, could we have perpetrated, encouraged, and spread the reprehensible evil we did? We now look at the Bible's six or seven fleeting mentions of homosexuality, and are astounded that we ever dared claim them as evidence that God cannot abide the gay and lesbian people whom He so lovingly created and sustains.

How could we have ever done such a thing? What, in the name of God, were we thinking?

Why were we moved to with such ferocious vigor supplant God's healing light with our own wretched darkness?

Our repentance demanded of us that we tirelessly ask ourselves that question—and keep on asking it, until we arrived at its answer.

And so we did.

The reason that we have so hated you is because we have so feared you. We feared you because we fear our own sexuality. We fear our own sexuality because its power seems to us far beyond what we are capable of controlling: so utterly, quickly, and inevitably does our sexual lust transform us from pious, composed believers into fevered, bucking animals.

Like *all* people (we now see, praise God), there are two natural phenomena that, in the overwhelming magnitude of their power, finally render us insensible of ourselves: the awesome presence of the divine infinite, and sex. We have always believed those two to be in competition, to be mutually exclusive. Traditionally our conviction has been that where God is, sex cannot be. And so we have always, if grimly, shunned our sexuality, and clung fast to God.

And there you are, out and proud.

There you are, embracing that within you which we can barely acknowledge in ourselves.

There you are, consciously, purposefully, and wisely integrating your sexuality into the whole of your identity.

There you are, with an audacity we now find inspiring and humbling, daring to believe that you, just as you are, are worthy of the most supreme love.

You joyously claimed the rainbow; while we, mired in our stubbornness, insisted on seeing only blacks and whites.

But now! Now has the terrible veil been mercifully lifted from our eyes! And therefore do we come before you today—repentant, ashamed, mortified to behold our transgressions against you—seeking not your forgiveness (for we would not dare), but only the slightest chance of proving to you that we have changed.

God *can,* after all, change hearts. And he has most certainly changed ours.

It might take a year for you to consider us your true brothers and sisters. It might take five years, or ten. It might take generations. But however long it takes, we promise you one thing: as of this day, the Christian church has renounced—and will forever, and with utmost vigor, continue to renounce—that wicked, vile, and manifestly false theology which holds you as anything but our equals and our friends.

With God as our witness, we will reconcile ourselves to you. That bright new day, so long in coming, has finally dawned.

With all that we are and hope to become,

Christians of the World

About the Author

John Shore is an award-winning book author who writes the immensely popular blog JohnShore.com. His seminal work on the relationship between LGBTQ people and Christianity has been featured on *Savage Love, The Huffington Post, The Dish, Advocate.com, GLAAD, Joe. By. God, LGBTQ Nation, Believe Out Loud, Truth Wins Out, The New Civil Rights Movement, Good As You, Towleroad, Box Turtle Bulletin, The Center for Progressive Christianity, The Christian Left, Crosswalk.com, Christianity.com, The Christian Post* and others.

A pastor ordained by The Progressive Christian Alliance, John is also the founder of Unfundamentalist Christians.

Made in the USA
Middletown, DE
07 September 2018